Leek
Westwood Hall
Girls' High School
1921-1965

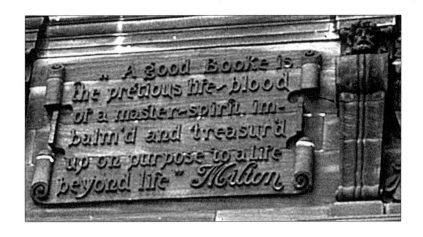

Anne & Brian Lewis

CHURNET VALLEY BOOKS
1 King Street, Leek, Staffordshire. ST13 5NW 01538 399033
www.leekbooks.co.uk
© Anne and Brian Lewis and Churnet Valley Books 2011
ISBN 9781904546771

This book is dedicated to all those whose lives have
been touched by the spirit of Westwood
and to our grandson Thomas Lewis Charles Foster

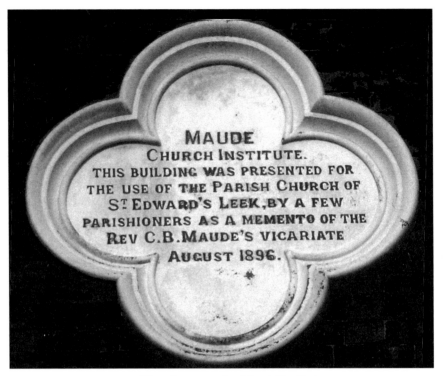

The plaque on the Maude Institute

ACKNOWLEDGEMENTS

Sincere thanks go to the following people and organisations, without their help this
book would not have been written.

Jennifer Amison; Jean Askey; Enid Ball; Gay Battersby; Brenda Beniston; Sheila Bettany;
Trudy Blood; Anne Biddulph; Hilary Brown; Geoff Browne; Julie Buxton; Jane Buxton; Jill
Coulthard; Dorothy Davies; Keith Davis; Pat Davis; Susan Davis; Jalna Edwards; Joan Fleet;
Barbara Fishburn; Margaret Fishwick; Jean Forrester; Gwen Giddings; Hilda Hassall; Anita
Hill; Keith Hollins; Doris Howson; Janet Hughes; Barbara Hutchinson; Norma Jones;
Gerald Mee; Ruth Milner; Hilary Ogden; Sam Plank; Mary Przyrembel; Pauline Raistrick;
Trevor Raistrick; Audrey Rennie; Bruce Richardson; Peter de Sausmarez; Ann Senior;
Mavis Stanley; Betty Ward; Gillian Willett; George Wiskin; June Wrathall;

Hampshire County Record Office Winchester, Hanley Library and Archives, Leek Library,
Leek Post and Times, The Sentinel, Staffordshire County Archive, Leicester County Record
Office, Werrington Library; St. Edward's Church, Leek.

Contents

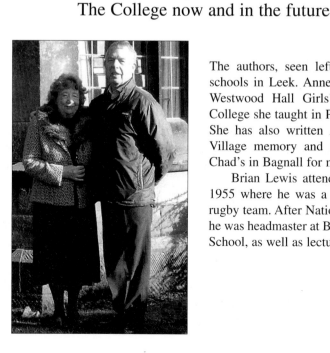

The authors, seen left, were both pupils at secondary schools in Leek. Anne Lewis (nee Bainbridge) attended Westwood Hall Girls' School from 1948-1956. After College she taught in Primary Schools in Stoke-on-Trent. She has also written *Bagnall Memories*, a School and Village memory and she was the churchwarden at St Chad's in Bagnall for many years.

Brian Lewis attended the Boy's High School 1948-1955 where he was a prefect and captain of the school rugby team. After National Service in the RAF and Aden, he was headmaster at Bradwell High and Wolstanton High School, as well as lecturing at Cauldon College.

Foreword

by the Executive Headteacher of Westwood College

I am both pleased and honoured to be asked to contribute to this book about the history of Westwood College. The timing of the production of the book is perfect, as the college prepares to celebrate the 90th anniversary of the founding of the school in 1921.

Throughout its long and proud history, the college has always valued individuals and individualism. One constant factor, over ninety years of constant change, has been the fact that each generation of young people has been able to attend a school where successive headteachers have subscribed to the view that the school's values should be built upon sensitivity, tolerance and the appreciation of difference. At the heart of the school's work has been the education of the young people in its care.

The ethos of the school has had an unswerving commitment to ensuring that all the students have an equal chance to make good use of the education that the school has offered, in order to help them choose their future patterns of life and take full advantage of their opportunities in society. To do this the school has always sought to develop personal confidence, study independence, the ability to make and sustain fulfiling relationships, flexibility, as well as the skills for the world of work.

There can be few buildings in Leek that are as iconic as the Old Hall at Westwood College. A school, however, has to be more than just a collection of buildings and throughout its history staff have sought to foster commitment to Westwood by parents, students, governors and others in the community, so that they will work for its development. This commitment, too, has been a constant theme binding together the successive generations that have attended the school. Rarely can a school, and its buildings, have generated such a strong feeling of attachment from its community.

The next few years are going to be ones of uncertainty in the public sector, and schools will not be immune from the changes that are going to take place due to spending cuts and policy decisions at local and national level. Our recent achievements bear testimony to the successful collaboration that exists between Westwood College, its students and their parents and carers and our wider community.

The current position of strength that the College finds itself in, as it enters this period of change, has its foundations in the efforts of the successive generations of people that have worked tirelessly to make this college the exciting place it is in which to work and study today.

Keith Hollins

Chapter 1

Early History of the Westwood Estate

When old girls, staff, parents and visitors remember Westwood their initial thoughts are not only about what went on in the classrooms, but about the grounds, the woods, the cedars, the lawns, the drives, the hall, the lodges, in fact the estate. All those who went to the school to gain an education and enjoy its delights owe a debt to those who had owned and developed this domain. It is worth considering the many who were fortunate to live and manage this estate throughout many centuries from the Norman Conquest to the present day. They would build, modify, demolish and rebuild. Their agricultural and building practices would develop this lovely area of Leek into what we know today.

In 1093 the Westwood Estate belonged to the Earls of Chester. Over a century later in 1214, Ranulph de Blundville, the 6th Earl, endowed the Cistercian Abbey of Dieulacres with part of the estate lands. The subsidy roll of Edward III, drawn up in about 1340, showed John de Westwood paying a tax of 12d. In the Dieulacres Abbey's dissolution list, drawn up prior to its closure in 1538, Westwood's entry read:

> ltem ye hamlet off ye lorde, coteying in yt brycholt Westwood and Woodcroft wt certeyn messes, landes, tentes of ye yerely value of xiiij oo viij.

Following the dissolution, the main tenants of the estate included Sir Ralph Bagnall in the early 17th century and Sir Francis and Lady Katherine Trentham of Rochester. In 1666 the house was taxed for seven hearths and must have been a substantial property. The Trentham family, who were one of the most important in the county, lived at Westwood for most of the 17th century. By the 18th century it was in the hands of the Jolliffe family of Caverswall Castle. On the death of William Jolliffe in 1709 the estate passed to his daughter Lucy.

In his *History of the Ancient Parish of Leek*. Sleigh tells how Lady Tempest Vane was killed jumping a double gate near to the top lodge and was buried in the cellar at the hall. The local clergy had trouble laying her ladyship's ghost. Long after Westwood became a school the girls would still recount the story of Lady Tempest Vane's ghost. This is how Joan Kennedy told the tale in the School magazine:

THE WESTWOOD GHOST
They say there's a ghost at Westwood Hall
The stone house shadowed by old, tall trees,
There wanders the ghost of Tempest Vane
Searching to find her lover again.
She restlessly passes from room to room,
Then disappears in the cellar's gloom,
Where she was buried to hide the shame
That elopement brought to the family name.

In 1759 Lady Vane's son, William Vane, sold the estate to Mary, Countess of Stamford. Her descendants, the Greys, retained Westwood until 1813. In that year it was sold to John Davenport, a potter and glass maker from Longport. Ownership had moved out of the hands of landed families to those of a self-made man. John Davenport was a native of Leek. Initially he had worked at Kinnerley's bank in Newcastle, but left to work in the pottery industry and subsequently founded his own works at Longport. He made sufficient money so that in 1813 as a widower with five children he could purchase Westwood from the Hon. William Grey.

At this time the house was described as an old Elizabethan house in a dilapidated condition. John decided to have the house remodelled and employed James Eames as his architect. They added a new South entrance and a wing to the North East. The enlarged house had two storeys with attics in the Elizabethan style boasting curved gables and mullioned and transom windows. The work on the house was undertaken during the 1820s and by 1834 the landscaped gardens were finished. After many years in Parliament, John retired in 1841 aged 76. The *Staffordshire Advertiser* in December 1848 printed his obituary:

> '*He entered the Potteries as an almost friendless youth but he had resolute determination and industry on his side and he lived to attain the summit of commercial eminence and fortune.... his favourite estate of Westwood is an instance of judicious application of capital to agriculture. Thriving plantations and fruitful fields cover hundreds of acres, which not many years ago were comparative sterile waste.*'

John Davenport junior born in 1799 inherited his father's estate. He decided to alter Westwood Hall still further and instructed the architects' partnership of Weightman, Hadfield and Goldie to design a new south elevation, a grand banqueting hall and a gothic type tower. They were also instructed to remodel the large dormers and to add an imposing entrance. The staff bedrooms were to be in the attics. He requested the whole of the South and East facades to be refaced with warm sandstone and some of the cellars were to be bricked up. At this time the size of the property could be estimated by the fact that there were now 40 fireplaces in the various rooms. In half a century John Davenport and his son made Westwood Hall and the estate into what we recognise today.

Pevsner in his book about Staffordshire described the hall as being a grand home of 1850-3 built on an older site. He thought it was a large irregular pile, gabled and ball - finialled, originally around two courtyards, although one had disappeared in later alterations and extensions. The unusual and rather unsatisfactory plan pointed to John Davenport's growth of ideas as the building progressed. The front was reminiscent of a Cotswold manor, but enlivened on one side by a great arched tower surmounted by a gothic belfry. The sides and East front were faced with red sandstone, but otherwise all was brick. There was pretty leaded glazing where it survived, but he felt there were far too many chimneys. Pevsner continued by saying that the interior was disappointing, though there was a two storey great hall, and in the former dining room there was an exuberant Elizabethan style chimney piece dating from 1852. The entrance lodge dated from 1852 and had a great arch. In the grounds was a charming contemporary summer house.

In 1862 a detailed inventory of the house and of the estate was drawn up so that it could be put up for sale. In spite of all the work it failed to sell. So in 1866 it was leased to James Watt. Two years later in 1868 the hall and estate were sold to John Robinson. He had made his fortune in engineering becoming chairman of the locomotive builder, Sharpe Stewart. At one time he was the High Sheriff for Staffordshire. He used his knowledge and wealth to maintain the hall and grounds in good condition. He lived there for thirty-four years with his wife and four adult

Westwood Hall before the alterations of the 1850s.

A drawing of the proposed alterations.

Westwood Hall following the alterations.

There are four carved heads
in the entrance hall. -
All were recarved after the
fire of 1983.

children together with the servants. He died in 1902 and his wife Helen passed away six years later. A debt of gratitude is owed to the Robinson family for the money spent and work done on maintaining an estate in the style of the Davenports.

The front drive lodge.

In 1909 the remaining members of the Robinson family sold the estate to H.J. Johnson. At the time of the sale the hall, gardens and grounds comprised 96 acres. Henry Johnson's major internal alteration was the installation of a large pipe organ in the back hall. He encouraged local musicians to give recitals on this fine instrument. The year before he sold the estate, the organ was removed and eventually installed in Stoke Minster, St Peters. A plaque recorded that the organ was given in November 1921 in memory of his son and son-in-law killed in the Great War. The Johnson family only lived on the estate for twelve years, when they advertised the estate for sale in the spring of 1920.

In March 1921, part of the estate comprising the hall, the carriageway and the gardens was finally sold to Staffordshire County Council for £15,500. In the September of that year, Leek Westwood Hall Girls' High School was opened there.

The back drive lodge after recent extensions.

A social gathering at Westwood circa 1900.

H.J. Johnson seated on the front row of a family gathering.

The advertisement of 1920 for the sale of the Hall.

Leek Grammar School in the 19th Century.

Mrs Brindley's Day School c. 1900.

Chapter 2
Leek Church High School for Girls

The old grammar school on Clerk Bank was built for the Earl of Macclesfield in 1732. It provided secondary education for over one and a half centuries for boys and in later years a few girls. Its closure in 1900 was due to financial difficulties and lack of support. Other institutions developed quickly to fill the void.

Pupils at the Old Grammar School.

W. R. Kean

–The Grammar School–

At the turn of the Century religious and political tensions came to the fore. For many years there had been intense rivalry amongst the various denominations, aided by wealthy benefactors, in providing school places. This rivalry had ensured that Leek had sufficient elementary places and so never needed a school board. The fight for control of Secondary Education in the town was just as contested, as had been the provision of elementary education.

Now there were only two sides in the contest. The competition in the town largely mirrored the national debate, which was between the Established Church aided by the Conservative party

The Maude Institute and the old Grammar School.

LEEK
CHURCH HIGH SCHOOL FOR GIRLS.

FOUNDED 1900.

Recognised by the Staffordshire Education Committee for Minor C and Intermediate County Scholarships.

Governors:

REV. E. SPINK, R.D. (Chairman).

REV. W. BERESFORD.   REV. W. B. WRIGHT.

MR. J. CARTWRIGHT.   MR. H. J. JOHNSON.

MR. ANTHONY WARD, C.C. (Representing the Staffordshire County Council).

MR. C. WATSON, J.P. (Hon. Secretary and Treasurer).

Head Mistress:

MISS M. L. CLEAVER, B.A. (London).   Cambridge Teachers' Diploma, late Second Mistress at the Royal School for Naval Officers' Daughters, Twickenham.

Front cover of Church High School's prospectus.

and the Non-Conformists aided by the Liberals. What emerged from fundamental differences, over provision and control of Secondary Education, were two separate and different schools. The secular authorities provided secondary education for boys and girls at the Nicholson Institute. The Anglican Church responded by establishing their own Church High School at the Maude Institute. The Church authorities, to show continuity of girls' secondary education, employed Mrs Brierly and her staff who had run a high school in a number of premises including one in Russell Street. Initially pupil numbers were small, only 25, but by the end of the school year, 1901, the figure had reached 45. The four rooms in the Maude Institute were to prove increasingly inadequate as numbers increased.

Reports on the school came from the annual visit of an academic appointed by the University of Manchester's Examinations Board, but these visits were seldom little more than a social occasion. In the summer of 1909 His Majesty's Inspectors made a formal visit and their detailed and concise report was presented to Miss Potts, the Headmistress and the governors. Details were recorded of pupil numbers, fees, premises and equipment, teaching staff and their salaries, the curriculum and the governing body.

The total number of pupils on roll was 100 of whom ten were young boys and 90 girls of whom four had scholarships. Pupils could start in the kindergarten at 4 years. Only a few remained to matriculate, one pupil being 20 years old! Fees were paid in 3 termly instalments at the local bank. Pupils aged 4 to 8 paid £4.14. 6. increasing to £12.12. 0 for pupils over 14   The cost of

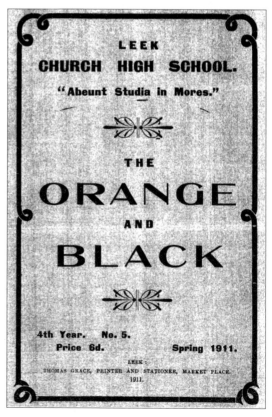

LEEK
CHURCH HIGH SCHOOL.

"Abeunt Studia in Mores."

THE

ORANGE

AND

BLACK

4th Year.   No. 5.
Price 6d.   Spring 1911.

LEEK:
THOMAS GRACE, PRINTER AND STATIONER, MARKET PLACE.
1911.

Front cover of the school magazine.

LEEK CHURCH HIGH SCHOOL FOR GIRLS.

Name....*Marian Hall*....   Form....$\overline{VI}^b$....

Term ending....**Dec: 17th 1909**....   Next Term begins....**Jan: 13th 1910**....

REPORT.

SUBJECTS.	Term.		Examinations.		REMARKS.		
	Maximum	Gained.	Maximum	Gained			
Holy Scripture } Prayer Book }	90	64			*Very good.* B.M.		**Conduct in School.** Order Marks lost 1. (ie 5 mks lost) Lessons neglected 0.
Arithmetic	60	56	100	78 }			
Geometry	100	90			*Very good indeed* L.S.		
Algebra	120	103					
Geography	60	48	100	55	*Very satisfactory*		**Attendance.** Absent, Morning 2
Composition					*Much improved*		Absent, Afternoon 4
History	80	58	100	43			Late, Morning 1 (excused)
Grammar	80	55 }	100	62	*Works well* B.M.		Late, Afternoon 0
Literature or Recitation	90	58 }					
Writing					*Good*		
Dictation					*Very good*		**Marks.**
Reading							Total Maximum 880
French	70	45			*Very good, on the whole* B.M.		Total Gained 723
German							
Latin							**Position.**
Science {Botany {Physical Geography {Heat, Light & Sound	80	69			*Very good* }	L.S.	Number in Form 4
	50	42					Place in Term's Work 2nd
Drawing and Brushwork							Place in Examination
Needlework							Final Place in Form
Excellents		40					
TOTAL	880	728	400	238			

Conduct and General Progress : *Very good Very Satisfactory*

Signed....*B. Fisher*....Form Mistress.   *Blanche W. Pott*....Head Mistress.

Marion Hall's school report of 1910.

stationery was 9/- for kindergarten pupils and 15/- for others. Parents had also to find money for school textbooks and uniform.

The Inspectors judged the premises with just four classrooms and a small cloakroom to be totally inadequate. Classes were observed being taught together in the same room. Physical activities took place on the playground when weather permitted; otherwise the kindergarten had to be moved to make room. There were no rooms for the headmistress or staff and there were only two toilets.

The school functioned with five teachers, the headmistress and a senior mistress who were both graduates supported by three former pupils of the school, two of who were still receiving tuition. Music and painting were taught by visiting teachers.

The curriculum reflected the school's position both as a Church and a grammar school. There was religious teaching from both the Old and New Testaments alongside Anglican doctrine, summed up as 'Definitive Church of England teaching'. As well as English there was French, German, Latin, and the head girl was learning Greek. Arithmetic was for all, and for those who progressed there was geometry and algebra. To complete a very extensive programme there were humanities and sciences:

Their final summing up was concise but not as forthright as it might have been:

Good discipline and organisation helps to cope with inconvenience arising from the defects of the premises. A more suitable building on a larger site needs to be considered by the governors.

It was to be more than a decade before a move was made. In spite of the acute accommodation problems the school seemed to flourish. Pupil numbers remained high ranging from 70 to 100 including a few boarders. However by 1917 the School's finances were in a poor state as expenditure exceeded income. The main problem was teachers' salaries. The hand written accounts for the Christmas Term showed a deficit of over £50. Financial help came from County Council funds with a subsidy of £150 per year. It was only to be a short time before Stafford took full and permanent control.

Miss de Sausmarez had only been Headmistress at the Church School for a few months when the County Education Authority, in 1919, decided to transfer the Church School, which it was subsidising, from independent status to that of a maintained secondary school. Control of the school was essential for future secondary education re-organisation plans. The name was changed to Leek Girls' High School, the word Church deleted, to emphasise the move from Church to local government control. After 19 years the independent Church High School ceased to exist, but there was continuity as Miss de Sausmarez was quickly appointed Headmistress and the new school remained in the old Maude Institute for another two years at an annual rental of £55.

In the High School's final year at the Maude Institute (1920-21) on the roll were 74 girls and two young boys of whom 25 were in the kindergarten and 51 in the main school. Fees ranged from £1.15.0 to £3.3.0 depending on age.

Chapter 3
The Struggle for Westwood

There were two letters to Sir Graham Balfour, Director of Education, at Stafford in the spring of 1920, both on the subject of purchasing Westwood Hall for a boys' school! They drew attention to the fact that building costs were high and the Hall and some of the land would be ideal. In the second letter was a copy of a page from the *Country Life Supplement* advertising 'The Westwood Hall Estate'. Sir Graham Balfour brought the matter of the possible purchase before his committee. Pressure was applied by the Board of Education and a decision to purchase was taken after a series of visits. Legal procedures ensured that the purchase was not completed until the following year. Accommodation had been a very serious problem at the town's two secondary schools for many years. It was particularly acute at the Girls' High School in the Maude Institute. The situation was only slightly better at Leek High School in the Nicholson Institute.

When the purchase of Westwood and the plans for its use were revealed to the public, Leek Urban District Council and the Society of Textile and Kindred Trades expressed objections and misgivings about the scheme. They argued that the proposed school would be a long way from the station. It was also 40 minutes walk from the centre of Leek and part of the route would be along lonely roads with no houses nearby. The site was certainly not satisfactory for the younger girls, as children would not have time to walk home for dinner and return to school in time for the afternoon session. The school would not actually be situated in Leek, but in an area known as Lowe. Alternative proposals were made. One suggested that a school should be built on land at the end of Beggar's Lane. This land was purchased but not used for nearly two decades

The opposition to the new school was so strong and vocal that a conference was held in Leek in July 1920. The County representatives were in favour of the new plan, the Leek representatives were against. The Rev Dunkley was in the chair. He informed all present that Westwood had been purchased. Nothing, he informed the conference had been decided other than the purchase and ideas for the use of the hall were sought.

The opposition repeated their earlier arguments about the location of the proposed school, the unsuitability of the buildings, the distance from the town and station and questioned as to why they were not consulted earlier. Measurements in yards were even taken from the station, the centre of town, the Nicholson Institute and even from the workhouse to Westwood to support their case.

The chair explained the committee's policy of locating secondary schools outside towns so that there was room for playing fields, which were essential. When the twelve members of the Education Sub Committee had visited the estate, any initial misgivings vanished and they eventually voted unanimously to recommend the purchase. The matter of cost was discussed further. Westwood could be purchased for £15,500 whereas to build a new school would cost £60,000. In an attempt to placate the opposition, a simple questionnaire was presented to parents seeking opinions on what to do with Secondary School education in the town.

At the end of September 1920 the Director of Education submitted his proposals for the reorganisation of Secondary Education. The plan was simple but radical, and consisted of four main sections:

The Nicholson Institute in 1900 showing to the right, the Leek Technical and High School - the Boys' School.

BELOW:

An early plan showing the Church Girl's High Schools' restricted site. (Now the Maude Institute)

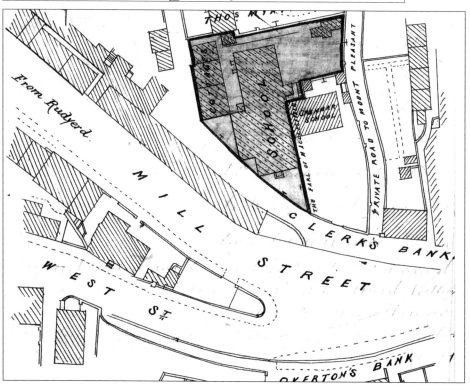

1. Leek Girls' High School premises to be vacated.
2. The two Preparatory Schools to be combined on the Leek High School site
3. Girls in both schools to be combined into one in the L.H.S. buildings
4. Boys from L.H.S. upper forms to go to the new school at Westwood.

The Board was quick in its response, agreeing with proposals I and 2 but not with proposals 3 and 4. The older girls, it directed, should go to Westwood and the boys remain temporarily at the Nicholson Institute with the combined Preparatory Schools.

What had swayed the argument was the number of girls in secondary education at LHS and LGHS in 1920 was 216 girls, compared with 145 boys. Girls outnumbered the boys on a ratio of 3 to 2 and future projection made the numbers even greater in favour of the girls. The Board of Education's proposals for reorganisation of secondary school education were accepted. In January 1921 the Board gave the school its name Leek Westwood Girls' High School and on 4th February the purchase of Hall and part of the estate was finally completed.

All the decisions had been made and the way for a major reorganisation for September was now open, but opposition to the proposed reorganisation was getting stronger. The opposition would not give up the fight and applied political pressure at Whitehall. In spite of the fact that Staffordshire's Education Committee had purchased Westwood Hall and agreed with the Board of Education that it was to be used as a girls' school, the whole matter was reviewed at a conference to be held in Leek on 22nd March 1921. Representatives of the Education Committee would meet with the Urban District Council.

The Director of Education was very concerned about the outcome of this meeting, fearing the worst. The meeting took place with the two sides, plus a Board of Education group, which included a barrister, an architect and an HMI. There were no new arguments put forward and the problem went back to Whitehall for a decision.

The Board replied that the objections put forward on distance and cost and the alternative schemes, did not afford reasons for withholding consent for Staffordshire's proposals. A rider was added that school should end by 3.30 pm in the winter and financial hardship over dinners should be addressed. The way was now clear for a new girls' secondary school at Westwood.

The East Wing of the Hall.

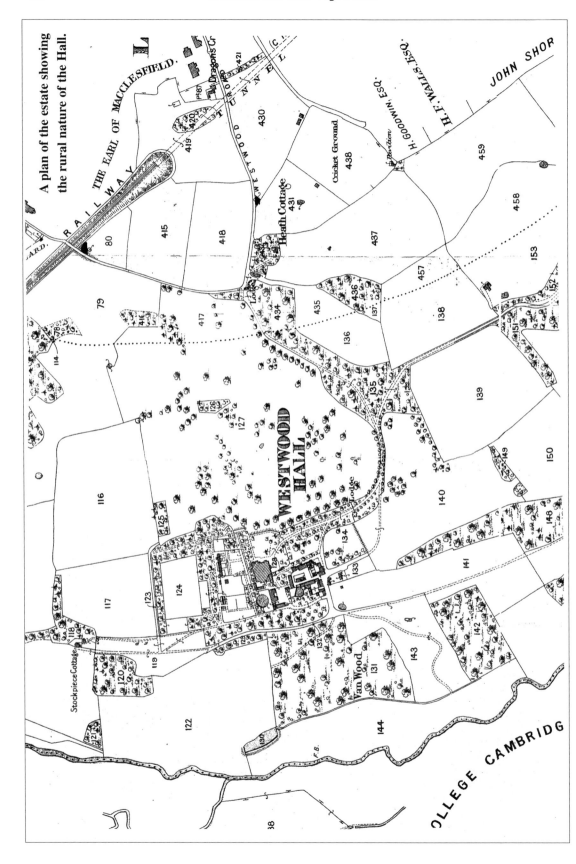

A plan of the estate showing the rural nature of the Hall.

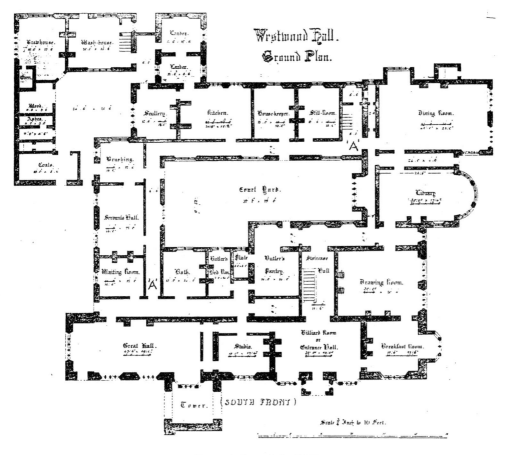

Ground plan of the Hall.

The stable block which became the caretaker's house.

The portrait of Miss E.F. de Sausmarez, headmistress 1921-1942, above the fire place in the front hall.

Below:
The front aspect of Sausmarez Manor, the home of Miss Elizabeth de Sausmarez' ancestors.

Chapter 4
Leek Westwood Hall Girls' High School

The site had been purchased, the buildings were there ready for modification, the next important step was to appoint a headmistress. The post was advertised in *The Education and Schools' World*. The advert made much of the size of the site, greatly overstated, and of the grand accommodation. Yet it was brief, to the point and read:

> *Headmistress is required for the Westwood Hall Girls 'High School Leek. The school will be opened in September next in a fine sandstone mansion in 94 acres of ground just outside Leek. Candidates must be graduates and have appropriate qualifications. Initial salary £500 rising to £640 (according to numbers). Headmistress appoints staff, salaries according to the Burnham Scale. Application to be made to Sir Graham Balfour, County Director of Education, not later than 2nd April 1921.*

Interviews were held and as expected, the senior mistress at Leek High School and the headmistress of the Church High School were interviewed along with other candidates. It was no surprise that Miss Elizabeth de Sausmarez, the Church High School headmistress, was appointed. She was highly qualified and experienced and well known to the governors and education committee members. Her curriculum vitae was exemplary. She was born in Acton, Middlesex on 2nd October 1885, the eldest of nine daughters, to Rev George Spencer and Fanny Maria de Sausmarez. She was awarded an MA in French at Lady Margaret Hall, Oxford. In 1909 she gained a London Teacher's Diploma at St. Mary's College, Lancaster Gate.

Her teaching experience was:

1909-1913 St. Mary's Abbots Bromley
1913-1915 North Foreland School, St Peter's in Thanet
1915-1918, St. Mary's Abbots Bromley (2nd Mistress)
1919-1921 Leek Church High School (Headmistress.)

The specially commissioned portrait of Miss E.F. de Sausmarez.

She received a letter from London later in April confirming her appointment as headmistress of the new school at Westwood from the date of opening.

A headmistress had been appointed, but the hall destined to be her new school was not ready. It needed many months of work on it and there were only five available before it was due to open. The manor building needed to be altered and adapted from that of a home for a gentleman and his family, to a school. Many changes were made but the physical structure was to remain largely untouched. Most rooms would remain too small for classrooms lacking, in many cases, adequate natural light.

It was decided that the school would consist of 10 classrooms, two laboratories, a dining hall and a gym as well as an assembly hall. The dining room of the old Hall was used as a combined dining room and assembly hall. This unsuitable arrangement

The summer house in its setting,
and below, a close up.

Left above: The clock tower.

Left below: The South side of the hall.

lasted for over three decades. Negotiations were made for an adequate water supply, which had to be pumped from Longsdon and for sewage disposal. The electricity supply and telephone service had to be upgraded and fuel supplies for heating arranged. The postal deliveries were to be left at the North Lodge. Kitchen staff, cleaners and a caretaker had to be appointed. Arrangements had to be made for the maintenance of the grounds and gardens and the entrance drive. These alone constituted a mammoth task.

Furniture needed to be ordered and by mid June 1921 new chairs had been purchased together with desks and teachers' desks. Some items were ordered from Harrods in London. The equipment needed for the gym in the entrance hall included a vaulting horse, jumping stands, spring boards and coconut matting. An extensive list was drawn up for the chemistry and physics laboratories; some of the furniture and benches were purchased from Loughborough College.

The recognition of Westwood as an efficient grant earning Secondary School was made on May 31st 1921. This new school would have repercussions elsewhere. The new school would not be open to junior girls, as it was considered too far out of town for them to walk there. They would all be accommodated in the Leek High School Prep School in the Nicholson Institute. This was not welcomed by all parents. Girls of the requisite standard and age would be transferred to Westwood. Fees would be payable at the same rates as those already applicable in each individual case. In 1922 the fees were 10 guineas a year (payable at £3.10s. per term) except for 25% of the girls who were awarded free places.

Preparations for the opening were delayed a little because the new headmistress took the long summer holiday with relations at Sausmarez Manor on the Isle of Guernsey. Numerous letters passed between Sir Graham Balfour, the Chief Education Officer at Stafford, and Miss de Sausmarez. She always wrote to Sir Graham in her distinctive, rounded handwriting on A5 sheets of paper with a black border.

The teaching staff at the two girls' schools awaited their future in the early months of 1921. A decision had been made in February to close the Church High School at the end of July and it was made clear to the staff that they were in no sense being dismissed. The staff based at the Nicholson Institute had to wait a few more weeks to see the plans for the amalgamation of the two schools finally approved. After she had been appointed headmistress Miss de Sausmarez was in a position to appoint the teachers. It was made clear that whenever possible graduates would be chosen. There would be ten full-time and three part-time teachers for September 1921. Six of the full-time teachers were from the Church School. The staff were:

Miss de Sausmarez (Headmistress),
Misses J. Carless, E. Malkin, E. Hulse, M. Page, M. Bearpark, K.Haywood, K.Shaw,
J.Curzen, M.Sant. Part timers were: E Phillips, W. Eaton, M. Brown

Miss de Sausmarez made everyone aware that the new school was a continuation of the old and in the admissions register started in 1921 the date of the girls' entry to the school is shown as that of the previous school. Pupil number one is recorded as having been admitted in 1913.

There was a prospectus to write and publish. Pupil selection policy had to be drawn up and made public along with criteria to select the 25% scholarship girls. Arrangements had to be made to collect fees and follow up non payment. School uniform requirements had to be issued, so that parents could make what would prove for many to be expensive purchases. A school badge and motto were needed. And following the many protests over the distance that many pupils would have to travel, it was essential to get dining arrangements right.

Jrnk Westwood Hall Girls High School. School.   No.1.

Surname _Minnison_   Christian Names } _Frances Alda_   Sex

Name of Father or Guardian }

Postal Address

1. Date of Birth.			8. Place of Residence.		9. Occupation of Father.	10. Place or places of previous education during the two years preceding
Day	Month	Year	County Borough or County		_County Surveyor_	_home_
17	9	05	_Staffs_			
2. Date of Admission.			and			
Day	Month	Year	(a) Borough or			
29	4	13	(b) Urban District _Jrnk_			
3. Date of Leaving.			or (c) Rural Parish			
Day	Month	Year	11, Particulars of any exemption from Tuition Fees.		12. Particulars of any Public Examinations passed or Certificates obtained while in the School, with dates.	
29	7	24	(a) Total Exemption.	(b) Partial exemption.		
4. Position on Admission.			Granted from (Date). _Sept: 1920_ _(Exhibition)_	Granted from (Date).	_Oxford Senior Local. Pass. July 192_	
					Letter of Success. Higher Certificate	
					of Northern Universities. July, 1924	
5. Position on Leaving.			Granted by (Body awarding). _Staffs C.C._	Granted by (Body awarding).		
6. Boarder or Day Scholar.				Annual Amount		
_D_			Tenable for _3 yrs_	Tenable for		
7 Terms kept.						
Autumn	Spring	Summer	14. Scholarships or Exhibitions for further education.	15. Place of further education.	16. Occupation taken up after leaving.	17. Remark
				Leeds University		

First entry in Westwood's admissions register dated 1913.
This was the admission date on which Frances started at the old Church High School.

The curriculum laid down in the School prospectus followed the guide lines issued by the Board of Education for Secondary Schools. The subjects offered were R.I. English, History, Geography, French, Latin, Maths, Science, Drawing, Class Singing, Cookery, Needlework, P.E. and Games. The girls were expected to aim for the Oxford School Certificate and the Higher School Certificate of the Northern Universities, although many left before sitting any examination.

The fees set were £3.10.0 per term and included stationery. All the girls were expected to take part in drill and games unless forbidden by a medical inspector. In those days there was no provision made for showers for the girls to take after their physical activities.

The school's own entrance examination had to be devised. All girls seeking a place were required to sit papers in Arithmetic and English with general questions on sentence analysis and composition. Girls needed to answer questions on *A Book of Verse for Boys and Girls* and *The Tanglewood Tales* - the choice was to vary from year to year. There was a viva voce examination followed by the written papers based on Geography and English History.

A quarter of the girls were then offered scholarships depending on the results. Having been granted a place either as a fee paying pupil or by a scholarship, an extensive school uniform list was issued. Each girl was required to have a navy blue drill tunic and school blazer or a dark blue jersey in winter. A school hat and hat band had to be worn. The hat band could be worn on a navy blue or black hat in the winter and a white straw or panama in the summer. A plain white dress was needed for school functions. Girls required a pair of indoor shoes and a pair of drill shoes to be kept at school. A special badge was designed for the school. The School motto which was not chosen until 1925, was part of a verse from the Bible, *With Goodwill Doing Service*. Many others were considered, usually in Latin, but the motto chosen was in plain English.

The thorny issue of school dinners was resolved with hot dinners provided at a cost of 8d a day. Girls who brought their own lunch could buy cocoa or hot milk. As required by the Board of Education, periodical medical inspections were given to all pupils and new girls were examined on entry to the school.

Even though there were still many problems to be resolved, in September 1921 the school opened with 140 girls taking their initial walk up the long drive to Westwood. Most of the girls on that first day had never been on the estate before. They were amazed by what they saw. A very young Anne Fowler recorded her observations in a piece entitled *First Impression of Westwood Drive:*

After the bustle of the busy streets, Westwood Drive seems to me as a cool and shady lane. It is long and winding and rather steep. The lovely old trees overhang it and make a very pleasant walk. I pass between green meadows and through a large gate into the grounds of Westwood itself. Here the sides of the drive are thick with rhododendron bushes, some as tall as trees, which are lovely in the spring. As I pass down the drive I see smooth green lawns and stately cedar trees and the handsome buildings of Westwood Hall standing majestically in the sunshine.

Miss de Sausmarez, in her final speech in 1942, explained that there had never been an official opening of the school, as there had been so many difficulties to overcome in that autumn term of 1921. She related that the only furniture in some of the classrooms was a kitchen table and a single chair. When the furniture eventually arrived the pupils seemed sad at the changes. Only the teachers seemed pleased.

Miss Carless, after she had retired, was asked to write about the early days. In an article for the school magazine, she looks back and describes the many problems encountered before and after the school first opened:

We started with 100 (pupils), I believe, and we had plenty of space. What we did lack was furniture and ordinary school equipment We had about 50 desks - three old blackboards, well painted up to look their best, and three shaky easels - one tied together with string. The fifty desks and blackboards were given to the younger children downstairs, the rest of the forms had chairs and when writing had to be done the girls had to kneel on the floor.

There were no dining tables. The girls sat on the floor and Miss Sant went round with a jug of cocoa. There was no heating but it had been a beautiful summer and the autumn was warm- there were trenches all along the passages, but fortunately everyone went about in an orderly manner, and nobody had a broken leg. There were ladders everywhere, and the worst thing that happened in connection with those, was that one brave girl appeared on the roof of the Laboratory. Great excitement, but nothing worse! There were also workmen everywhere, and we had to teach with a background of whistling and singing.

Two schools were amalgamated to make Westwood, and there had of course been a great deal of discussion as to how the girls and the staff would settle down together. We did settle down so well that the parents were astonished to hear that work had begun immediately and that their children had for homework nineteen sums and forty pages of history.

Towards half term the weather became colder, and then the workmen decided that it was time to remove the windows, which had to be replaced with plain glass and ventilators, so we had fires in the form rooms and a line chalked on the floor beyond which of course no child thought of going. The girls were good in those days! The classes of course were much smaller, and the players of tunes on pins stuck in the desks which eventually arrived, were easy to detect.

The autumn term in 1921 had started late because the building was not ready, but a week before the girls arrived, the staff had been enjoying themselves, clearing the school and, incidentally getting to know each other.

By 1923 there were 146 girls at the school but two years later the numbers had dropped to 132. Each year concern was expressed at governors' meetings about the number of girls who had requested to be released from attending school before they had reached the age of sixteen. The headmistress also had to address the growing problem of late and non payment of school fees.

Miss Carless with the girls.

A group in 1934 with Jean Trafford on the far left.

There were various reasons given. Often there were financial difficulties or there was a serious illness in the family and help was needed at home or the girl had been offered employment. Miss de Sausmarez spent a considerable amount of time writing letters to the families concerned, refusing to release the girls and pointing out that they were expected to remain at school until they were 16 years old. In one instance a girl had been offered employment as a librarian in Leek. The headmistress had to write to the girl's father to inform him that he must pay £5 for liquidation damages and if he refused, the clerk of the County Council would take proceedings.

She had to write letters to parents explaining that as no fees had been paid, their child would have to leave the school and arrangements must be made for their daughter to be admitted to an elementary schools in the area, as there was still an obligation for her to continue her education. Sometimes the local solicitors Bowcock and Pursaill were called upon to help to resolve financial matters. For over two decades, the twin problems of non payment of fees and requests that girls be allowed to leave school before they were sixteen, were a constant problem.

The Headmistress was required by the Education Committee to find suitable lodgings in Leek for girls who found it difficult to travel. The rents for these lodgings were paid by the Education Authority. Travel expenses were also paid for all girls living outside the Leek area and they received their travel warrants each term.

The headmistress also dealt with requests for the use of Westwood for courses during holiday times. One of the first was for a course on Rural Science for Elementary Teachers. She had to provide accommodation for 26 men in single beds together with the halls, the music room, the laboratories, playing fields and tennis courts. Beds and equipment had to be borrowed and the caretaker and cooks had to be persuaded to take on extra duties. The Governors and Miss de Sausmarez agreed and a successful course ensued. In 1923 a summer camp for girls was also held at school with tents pitched in the grounds. Other courses and camps followed.

There were the problems of the estate to be dealt with. School life was never placid or simple. There was a complaint from the tenant of Westwood Hall Farm because some of the fences surrounding the school grounds were in a poor condition. These were the responsibility of the school. Some of his stock had wandered through the broken fences and had been poisoned by the yew on the school premises. Consequently negotiations had to be held with the Governors and Staffordshire County Council to repair the boundary fences.

Miss de Sausmarez felt that it was important for the girls to appreciate works of art and to be surrounded with beautiful things. In 1936 she made a request to borrow art work from the Victoria and Albert Museum in London. The Headmaster at Leek School of Art arranged to visit the museum on April 13th, to select works for both his school and for Westwood.

The school commemorated two significant royal occasions. When King George V and Queen Mary celebrated their silver jubilee in 1935, the town put on a procession of floats, like a carnival. Westwood's float was of the Burghers of Calais. The participants were appropriately dressed, with soldiers in silver painted dishcloths to represent chain mail, and the embattled burghers in moth-eaten bits of fur, cotton wool and curtaining. In 1937 the school took part in a procession through the town to celebrate the coronation of King George VI. Both the pupils' uniform and the school's float was said to be eye-catching.

Mary Jepson (1932-39 (Mrs Przyrembel) remembers other facets of school life during this time.

I was one of a small group of 9 year olds, who passed the entrance examination from Leek Kindergarten. On our first day we walked up the long drive to Westwood feeling rather nervous. Our group was on average over a year younger than the other new girls from other schools. Our classroom was small and off the entrance hall which was the gym and also used for music lessons and country dancing. Miss de Sausmarez's office was nearby. Each morning lines of girls attended Assembly for prayers and a hymn before lessons started. The headmistress and the prefects were on a platform. None of the teachers was young, apart from the gym mistress, and that remained the same for all the time we were there. They were dedicated and good at their job and were respected by us. We were very well behaved in those days, (most of the time at any rate).

I remember chemistry, physics, biology and botany lessons in the labs. There were no fridges in those days and the rabbit we studied really smelt awful. (We were allowed to put our hands over our noses).

Speech days took place each year at the Town Hall, where book prizes were given out to the best pupils. We also had occasional lectures there together with the Boys' High School, the boys would sit on the left of the hall and the girls on the right. We had a girl guide troop which met after school.

Our school field was where the housing estate is now. We had teams which played other schools on some Saturday mornings. We played rounders, netball, hockey and tennis. I was in all of them and I have always enjoyed sports. Those wanting to play tennis would often play after school. The courts were on the lawns.

We were being educated and prepared for adult life, so cookery and needlework were very important too. In those days not so many of us went on to further education as they do now. Westwood was a very good school

Kathleen Porter 1922-29 (Mrs Mason)

I went to Westwood School in 1922 when I was 10. At the time there were no houses at all anywhere in the area and the road from Westwood Heath went under the archway of the bottom lodge. From there on it was woods on either side, carpeted with bluebells in Spring.

Part of the 1928 School photograph. On Miss de Sausmarez' left is Miss Carless & Miss Greenstreet. Miss Ashworth is the first teacher on the left.

Halfway up the drive on the left hand side was a side road which came out on Newcastle Road near to Westwood Golf Links. Girls who lived at Longsdon and beyond used this road to get to school.

We walked on past the second lodge on the left and then by the back drive past Plant's Farm to school. We were never allowed to use the front drive.

The teachers had a shorter walk from the bottom lodge to a gate by the old Summer House - there is an old well not far from there. Miss de Sausmarez (who we called Sammy) and Miss J.W. Carless (who we called John Willy) came to school everyday in a taxi.

When I first went to school we were living in Bath Street and I used to walk to school with Margaret Bessie Bowers who lived in Ford Street. There were 19 girls in my form; at the time there would be no more than 120 girls in the whole school.

We had Prize Giving (Speech Day) every year in the Autumn in the Town Hall. I still have five of the programmes from 1923 to 1927. In 1923 the address was given by Tom Hassall Esq and the prizes presented by Sir Arthur Nicholson. In 1924 Sir Arthur gave the address.

Generally a small play was performed by some of the girls and then the Headmistress gave her annual report. Songs were sung usually including a patriotic one like 'Jerusalem', 'This Sceptered Island' or 'O England, My Country'.

The first head girl was Alda Rinnison, a natural platinum blond and very pretty. They lived at Abbey Green.

We wore round caps or green hats with a flat turn-up back and front, with a red badge embroidered on the front. In summer we had either a panama or straw hat with narrow bands of red, green and white stripes. We were not allowed to walk through town without a hat or cap on and were certainly not allowed to eat anything in the town wearing our school uniform.

In the lower forms we played netball in the Winter and rounders in the Summer. The older girls played hockey in the Winter and cricket in the Summer. These games were played on a field near to the square. There were three tennis courts and in Summer girls could stay on after school to play, and we paid 3d for tennis tea after.

In 1938 it was agreed that some of the land by the school lodge should be developed and that the private school drive, was to become a public road. Miss de Sausmarez was concerned about these changes, and the affect they would have on pupils' safety. She requested a local bus service from the bottom lodge into Leek which would be of great benefit to town girls and country girls who had to catch buses from the cattle market. This request was not granted until many years later.

Physical Education was an important part of the curriculum. There had been little provision for outdoor games so a nearby field belonging to the local farmer, Mr. Plant, was leased. In 1935 this arrangement was considered unsatisfactory so an area at the north end of the school site was developed as a new playing field. Bakers of Wolverhampton gained the contract to excavate, level, drain and seed the area. The project cost was £1,250 and in the following year a part time grounds man was employed to work on the field. Sadly it was another 5 years before the area was declared fit for use.

Staffing for physical training was always a problem in the early years. For a number of years a teacher shared her time between Westwood - 3 days and Uttoxeter Girls' High School - 2 days. As P.T. and games became a more important part of the curriculum the sharing ceased and a full time P.T. teacher was employed.

1932 SCHOOL PHOTOGRAPH.

1936 SCHOOL PHOTOGRAPH.

Hilda Burchell 1934 -1940 (Mrs Hassall) remembers P.T. and Games lessons.

I went to Westwood in 1934 when Miss de Sausmarez was the head mistress. In those days our summer uniform was a cotton gym slip or pinafore dress with a white cotton blouse. We

Girls in the 1930s.

changed our shoes on arrival at school for indoor ones, and we also had pumps for gym which took place in the Entrance Hall and rather cramped our style in Horse and Box exercise. Our lessons were often interrupted for visitors. In the summer we also played tennis. We played hockey and netball, but not on the present games field, which was a later development -but on the field beyond the Summer House. I think there are houses there now. The pitch was on a slight slope and dotted with rabbit holes, down which the ball frequently strayed. We used to play other High Schools like Brownhills and Thistley Hough. We would serve refreshments, sometimes toast and dripping which was very good.

One of the girls, who later in life became my sister-in-law, used to organise conducted tours of the roof in the lunch hour. The roof was strictly out of bounds and I never went, but friends of mine who did said that it was very scary! Miss Carless discovered them and, of course, that was the end of that.

We had a school guide company which was started by Miss Walker who was the head of English. We were divided into patrols, each named after a bird. We went

The Mad Hatter from the 1930s
'Alice in Wonderland'.

'The Spinsters of Lush' performed during the 1930s.

Hilda Birchall second from the right, Mary Jepson second from left.

camping on the Buxton Road where the new cemetery is now and we learnt to play cricket.
Some of us became Queen's guides.

As well as sport we were encouraged to get involved in drama. Our best production was
a play entitled 'The Spinsters of Lush.'

When in 1939 the new Boys' High school opened in Westwood Road, it began a fresh debate about building a brand new school to replace Westwood where the accommodation was still considered to be below that required of a modern secondary school. The Director of Education was against any move on financial grounds. He argued that a considerable amount of money had been spent on the girls' school. The Westwood estate had cost £15,500 to purchase and another £4,000 had been spent on adapting it for school use. Since then minor improvements had been carried out costing approximately £2,000. The £21, 000 already spent would have been wasted and the cost of building a new school was in the region of £35,000.

The financial consideration far outweighed other arguments and a decision was made not to close Westwood. Accounts were published for the next three years showing that, even in a period of austerity, costs kept rising. In 1940 there were 212 girls in the school and 36 in the preparatory department. The gross expenditure for the school during the year 1938/1939 was £4,947 and by 1942 the gross expenditure had risen to £5,724.

From September 1939 this country was at war with Germany and the possibility of bombing raids on our major cities was a growing concern. Preparations were made for school children together with their teachers to be evacuated from Manchester and Kent to Leek. A number of the evacuee children attended the preparatory school, in the huts at the Nicholson Institute and arrangements were made for older evacuees to attend Westwood. As the phoney war period lengthened many of the evacuees drifted back home and only a few were to spend all the war years here.

Hilda Burchell 1934-40 remembers the war years.

The school dinners were excellent and we learnt good table manners. Miss Sant, our cookery
and needlework teacher, was in charge of the catering for the meals, and there were large

joints of meat carved by members of the staff and scrumptious puddings to follow. This did not continue when war broke out although we still had good, nutritious meals and did not suffer as some people did.

During the war years we took gas masks to school each day. The air raid shelters were situated behind the school near the playing field. We only used them once when we were in the sixth form. We heard a siren and assumed it was from Leek. We crowded into the shelters. In fact it was a very still day and the siren proved to be from Bullers at Milton, quite a few miles away. It must have been a very powerful one.

During the war years the girls at Westwood did not have to undertake fire watching duties - although the boys at Wolstanton Grammar School did - for a small remuneration. However, when I had left Westwood and was training to be a teacher in Edinburgh, my friend Brenda Tunnicliff and I returned to Westwood to visit Miss de Sausmarez. She asked us if we would help her out by spending the night in her study and look out for incendiaries falling on the roof and causing fires. We agreed to her request, but we fell asleep in the middle of the night and had to be woken up by the caretaker. I enjoyed my years at Westwood and later gave a cookery prize to be awarded at speech day each year.

Miss de Sausmarez assumed the responsibility for the Prep School in 1939, when the boys moved from the Nicholson Institute to the new premises in Westwood Road. She took her new responsibility seriously and made numerous journeys between Westwood and Stockwell Street. In 1942 she complained to the Education Authorities that her ration of one and a half gallons of petrol every three months was not enough to cover the distances involved.

Later that year one of the Westwood staff, Miss Greenstreet, applied for leave of absence to join the Red Cross as a nurse. The governors agreed to grant her request and to keep her post as a domestic science teacher open for her. At the end of the war Miss Greenstreet returned to the school to resume her teaching career.

Along with most schools in the country, Westwood supported 'Salute the Soldier Week' in May 1942. A target of £350 was set and easily surpassed. The efforts of many groups in the school were commended, particularly the Guide Troop. The final total raised was £516.12s

From the opening of the school there had always been problems in domestic science, as cookery was taught in the same kitchens the school dinners were prepared each day. A radical and unsatisfactory decision was made to move the domestic science department into the biology laboratory upstairs until a better arrangement could be made. It was a challenge to move the cookers and all the necessary equipment up the stairs to the laboratory.

After twenty one years at Westwood, as the first headmistress, Miss de Sausmarez tendered her resignation to take effect from December 1942. She resigned for domestic reasons, to care for her elderly mother. The governors agreed to her request with regret and expressed their appreciation of her services to Westwood since 1921. She had a long and well deserved retirement, living to the age of 96 years. Two ladies who were pupils in Miss de Sausmarez's time, share some of their memories and experiences.

Jean Forrester a pupil 1941-1949

I went to Westwood in 1941 aged 10, having passed the Special Place Examination. We went into IIIB with Miss Griffith as form and history teacher. I loved the lessons. The school was beginning to grow and so there was also a parallel IIIB. It was the first time there had been

more than one form in each year. As we progressed up the school pressure on space grew, as the only accommodation for the whole school was the old hall. Miss de Sausmarez was the head. She retired in my second year and was replaced by Miss Stanton. She taught us Latin with some modern methods such as writing and reciting, 'The house that Jack built' in that language -Haec est villa quae Jacobus aedificavir.

I couldn't draw and was an untidy writer so nature study was a nightmare and so was the art.

I don't remember the war having much impact except that it was difficult to get the light green material for the summer uniform. Uniform was strict and we were expected to change into indoor shoes. Fortunately various old girls passed on the Westwood green tunics which my mother altered for me. Much altering was quite common as coupons were short and for many of us, so was money. Milk was available at break from Plant's Farm nearby. I loved the setting of Westwood and never tired of the lovely grounds and gazing through the windows at the view of the Moorland Hills beyond Leek. I walked to school until I had a bike in my second year. Eventually I rode home at lunchtime. We were allowed to ride up and down the drive at lunchtimes but not in mornings and evenings. There were no houses then and, apart from lunch times we were supposed to walk from the bottom lodge but we did ride if we could get away with it. I remember walking to school in the winter in a navy gabardine coat: not waterproof. The 1947 winter, when I was in the Lower VI, was a challenge and lessons were disrupted. Some country girls couldn't get to school for five weeks. One day having struggled in, we were sent out with shovels to clear the drifts.

By the time I was in the Lower V Miss Stanton had left and Miss Bull was head until some years after I left. Other teachers I remember were Miss Beck, Miss Ashworth and Miss Phillipson as well as some lively younger teachers.

I remember May 8th 1945 when we went into the hall to hear Churchill announce that the war in Europe was over and there was a holiday next day. I remember a discussion before I went home whether we ought to do our Maths homework set during the day. Did the end of the war make a difference? Some of us did it and some did not, it did not matter as it was set again after the holiday!

There were History outings with Miss Griffith and visits to concerts in Hanley and of course Guides on Friday afternoons. There were lots of fun and gossip with friends and endless funny stories which we still relate when we meet.

We had some good teachers whose words I remember. I went on to read History at University and owe a lot to Miss Griffith who awakened my love of History and to Miss Ogilvy who taught us in the Upper VI.

Barbara Pilkington 1941-48 (Mrs Fishburn) recalls some teachers.

A few years ago I was invited to return to Westwood to talk to some history students about the school during the war. Miss de Sausmarez was the head teacher in 1941, when I started to attend Westwood. She was later succeeded by Miss Stanton and then Miss Bull. It was interesting to see how youngsters reacted to what I had to say. In 1941, the war had been on for two years. As well as our satchels we had to carry our gas masks to school every day. Many of the girls and boys travelled to school by train from Cheddleton, Oakamoor, Alton, Froghall and Ipstones; the boys went to Leek High School, then situated where St. Edwards

Middle School stands. The trains arrived at Leek station now Morrisons, and then the pupils had to walk to Westwood. At dinner time the whole school sat down together in the main assembly hall. The high table was positioned under the long window, we all remained standing until Miss de Sausmarez and the teachers came in. Then after she had said grace we were allowed to sit, eat and talk quietly.

The more eccentric members of staff are the ones I remember well. Miss Greenstreet who taught Domestic Science, still stands out clearly. She rented a room in the white house near to the lodge at the bottom of the front drive. She rode to school and back each day on her push bike. On rainy days she would ride with her umbrella held proudly above her head. Her memory wasn't very good and she often forgot things. In those days we would have cookery for a term followed by a term of needlework. One year she had taken delivery of all the needlework materials ready for the following term and she had stored them away safely. When the needlework term started she couldn't find the materials. Everyone searched high and low, eventually they were found at the back of one of the ovens. Fortunately no one had set fire to them. One of our needlework projects was to make a petticoat. When I had completed mine and took it home my mother (who was a dress maker) thought it looked like something from the 1920s.

In the cookery room, there was a walk-in cupboard used to store saucepans and other equipment. Any aluminium pans would have been sent to make' planes for the war effort, so we had heavy cast iron things. Sometimes a girl would go into the cupboard and knock pans off the shelves making a dreadful din. When Miss Greenstreet came to investigate the girl would cry and say it was an accident and she was sorry, but the pans had hurt! (Now, I can't imagine why we thought it was funny)

Miss Ashworth, who taught me Latin, and Miss Beck shared a house in Leek. I was quite a small school girl and when Miss Ashworth stood in front of me at the front of the class she looked so big and frightening with lots of hair. She was quite intimidating. One day she looked at me and called me out to the front. She wanted me to take a message somewhere for her. When I got outside the classroom I had felt so frightened I couldn't remember the message. I didn't know what to do. I thought about running home, but I knew my mother would have been so annoyed with me. I thought about going to hide in the wood, but in the end I decided there was nothing to do but return to Miss Ashworth and tell her that I had forgotten what I had to do. She glared at me when I explained my predicament. Then she said, "Sit down, I shall not ask you to do anything for me again." She never did!

The attics were out of bounds to the girls, but of course we were all fascinated to know what was up there. One day in 1943 we decided to investigate that area of the school. We explored what seemed to be endless fairly empty rooms. It was interesting to find lots of pottery, big ewers and bowls which had obviously been used to hold water on the dressing tables when Westwood had been a country house. There were even chamber pots and odds and ends of furniture. One former member of staff remembered seeing a beautiful roll topped desk in one the rooms and the stationery cupboard downstairs had once been the laundry room in the old house. The rows of shelves were still there. It was a glimpse of family life in years gone by.

Chapter 5

Miss K. M. Stanton,
Headmistress May 1943-December 1946

Following Miss de Sausmarez's resignation, advertisements for a new headmistress were placed in *The Times Educational Supplement* and *The Spectator*. The governors were quite surprised when they received 117 applications. Six candidates were selected for interview and Miss Stanton, who had been the headmistress at Basingstoke High School since 1935, was appointed on a salary of £700 pa.

Left: Believed to be Miss Stanton aged 34 when headmistress at Basingstoke High School.

Right: Miss Stanton after retirement aged 73.

Miss Stanton was born in Birmingham in 1902 and for seven years, 1914-21 attended King Edward VI School in New Street. At Newnham College Cambridge 1921-24, she was an outstanding scholar being awarded her MA and a distinction in Ancient Philosophy. Before coming to Westwood she had taught in Oldham, Leeds, Leicester and Basingstoke.

In January 1943 Miss Carless was acting headmistress for one term. In many ways she was Miss de Sausmarez's natural successor having worked with her for over twenty years as senior mistress, helping develop Westwood in its formative years. It is not certain whether or not she applied for the post. The governors appointed a younger woman with high academic qualifications who was an experienced headmistress.

Brenda Newbon 1943-1950 (Mrs Beniston) gives her memories of this time

Miss Stanton was the headmistress when I went to Westwood. I remember there were problems at dinner times trying to fit all the girls into the hall for lunch. Some of the girls had to eat their dinners in the kitchens where the meals had actually been cooked, and this arrangement caused a number of difficulties.

WESTWOOD HALL GIRLS' SCHOOL, LEEK

Name _Anne Mosley_   Form _III alpha_   Age _10.yr. 8m._

Report for _Autumn_ Term, 19_43_   Class _A_   Average Age _11yr. 9m._

Next Term begins _Tues. Jan. 11th_   Position _1._   Height _4' 8"_ Weight _5.st.10¾_

Next Term ends _Mar. 31st_   No. in Form _30_   Order Marks _!_

Times Absent _0_ Times Late _____   Returned Lessons _0_

REPORT

A—Very Good.   B—Good.   C—Fair.   D—Poor

TERMS WORK	1st Week	2nd Week	3rd Week	4th Week	5th Week	6th Week	7th Week	8th Week	9th Week	10th Week	11th Week	12th Week
WEEKLY CLASS	A	A	A	A	A	A	A	A				

SUBJECTS	Exams. percentage	REMARKS	Signature
Old Testament	87	Very good. Anne has worked well this term.	I.M.H.
New Testament			
English Grammar		Good work. The appearance of Anne's work has improved.	RB
Composition	83	Very good. Anne has done a very good examination paper.	I.M.H.
Writing		Good, on the whole.	
Dictation	63	Good	
Reading		Good.	
Literature		Very good.	
History	50	Good during the term.	M.G.
Geography		Good.	E.T.B.
Arithmetic	86		
Algebra			
Geometry			
French		Good. Anne works well.	D.C.D.P.
Latin			
Nature Study	59	Good on the whole.	P.G.W.
Physics			
Drawing		Very fair.	
Drill		Ann works well	ews.
Needlework			

Form Mistress' Report:

Conduct _Good._

Progress _Very good. Anne has worked well._

Head Mistress' Report: **Very good.**

Signed _I.M. Hallam._

Signed _K. R. Stanton._

Anne Mosley's school report of 1943.

Miss Stanton was very keen to encourage cultural visits. I recall going to the Victoria Hall in Hanley to an orchestral concert. We also visited the Theatre Royal in Hanley to see a ballet, but unfortunately the theatre was destroyed by fire the following day! We visited the cinema in Leek to see Lawrence Olivier in Hamlet, Omar Sharif in Lawrence of Arabia, and later we saw Scott of the Antarctic.

In 1949 when Miss Bull was the headmistress at Westwood, we had a school visit to Stans in Switzerland. Miss Bell and Miss Jones organised the visit and accompanied us. We found the scenery in Switzerland breathtaking. We visited the Rhone Glacier. It was quite a journey by coach for us and we were glad of rugs to wrap around us as we passed through the clouds at the top of the glacier. We also went for a trip on Lake Luzern and ascended the Stanserhorn Mountain by funicular railway. I hadn't been on a funicular before so it was quite an experience.

I shared a room with Anne Mosley and Pamela Rickett and that was great fun. However, I was really impressed by the fact that in Switzerland we didn't need coupons to buy sweets. In England sweets and chocolates were still on ration even though the war had ended four years earlier.

Miss Stanton brought changes to school life. Her stay at Westwood was a very short one of just eight terms. In this time she had many problems with the staff, largely confined to the non-teachers. Difficulties arose with the school secretary, the school cook, the caretaker and the local farmer. Shortly after she arrived she expressed her concern about the school secretary to the Director of Education. She felt that the secretary found the demands of her job too much to cope with. She felt that she would like a secretary who could cope with the secretarial duties and teach shorthand and typing to the girls. It is unclear whether or not her request was fulfilled.

In the new Headmistress's first year one of the gas cookers in the kitchen exploded. The gas department was called in but explained that the cooker could not be repaired and a new one would have to be purchased. The cooks were preparing 220 hot dinners each day and 45 cold meals. The explosion gave Miss Stanton the opportunity to remove the head cook who could not cope and set up a new non-teaching post, that of cook/ matron. The new job description with its multiplicity of responsibilities was as detailed and elaborate as that for the school secretary. Mrs Lucy Bennett was appointed as cook supervisor/ matron at a salary of £192 pa. Problems with cooking/dining arrangements are often mentioned by former pupils.

Beryl Tipper (Mrs. Haime), Freda Warrington (Mrs Fernyhough) and Audrey Shenton (Mrs Rennie) - all pupils 1943-1948/50.

When we started at Westwood one of us paid 2/3 of the fees, the other two didn't pay anything. The payers also had to pay for textbooks. There appeared to be a shortage of textbooks for some subjects. After the Education Act of 1944 none of the girls had to pay

It was very difficult at dinner times- there were problems attempting to fit all the girls into the dining areas. Some of us ate in the kitchens where the food was prepared. Miss Griffith, the history teacher, sat at one of the tables there and we had to rotate each week so that we took it in turns to sit by her. This was certainly one way for her to get to know us. The girls taking sandwiches had to eat them sitting on the stage in the back hall.

Of course when we started it was war time and it was difficult to obtain the school uniform -.we needed coupons. Clothes had to altered and lengthened and passed down through the family. One girl had a cardigan that had been lengthened on the sleeves and at the waist. Unfortunately the colour of the wool didn't quite match.

Sometimes if the weather was good we had gym outside in front of the school in our knickers, blouses and ties. We always thought it was funny to have to wear our ties! The boys from the High School would sometimes come to Westwood to join the girls for Biology and they usually came through the front door. When this happened, our P.E. teacher would tell us to sit on the ground until the boys had disappeared inside.

We remember going on strike one day. We hadn't been allowed to watch the juniors when they performed their plays in the dramatic competition, so we protested by standing outside in the courtyard. Miss Stanton was extremely annoyed with us and kept us in at break while she gave us a lecture on trade unions.

On another occasion we walked out of a music lesson. It appeared to be Miss Stanton's policy to encourage non-teaching staff to participate in school activities and one of the cooks was taking us for singing. We can't remember her playing the piano, but the lesson went very badly and we were getting more and more frustrated, so we simply walked out. We were in trouble again, and received more lectures from Miss Stanton.

Another accident was less dramatic, but illustrated one of the many different problems that the Headmistress faced. The father of one of her young pupils who had fallen while in school and broken her wrist, wrote to Miss Stanton. He felt that as it had cost him £10.10.0 (the exact school fee for the year) to have the bones reset by a doctor, he ought to be exempt from paying the school fees for the forthcoming year. The request was not granted by the governors.

The war continued to affect school life. The issue of fire-watching caused arguments and frustration within the staff. Miss Stanton was quick to point out that the teachers were doing their allotted 48 hours a month but there were still problems. She was unable to resolve a dispute between the caretaker and the local farmer who unilaterally declared that his fire watching duties would be confined to his own farm in future. The headmistress could not sort it out so she reported the matter to the local ARP headquarters and to the Education Office in Stafford.

The girls did their bit in the last years of the war, joining in the public appeal to invest in more national savings in 'The Wings for Victory' week in May 1943. Along with other Leek schools they put on a series of outdoor events including dancing and singing.

The war years also brought an interesting letter from an ex-pupil who had joined the Women's Royal Naval Service.

Women's Royal Naval Service Depot Essex 1944.

Dear Westwood,
It is rather difficult writing about life in the W.R.N.S. as you never know when to start, but anyhow, I will try.

We are billeted in a converted hotel on the edge of Epping Forest a very nice place to be, but not quite as nice as home. The rooms, or cabins, as we call them, are quite large, and there are usually about six girls in each one. We sleep in double decker bunks, which seemed very strange to us at first, but we soon got used to them. We have two studies where we can work at night, and a 'fo'c'sle that is a common room, where we can read or write or listen to the wireless.

As for our work, we get up at 6.15am and breakfast is at 7am, then we make our bunks and clean out our cabins etc. We muster outside the depot at 7.50 and march in squad to the trolley bus stop, about a mile away. The South West Technical College is about ten minutes ride away and we usually arrive there just in time to start work at 8.30am.

WOMEN'S · ROYAL · NAVAL · SERVICE

join the Wrens

AND · FREE · A · MAN · FOR · THE · FLEET

Wartime recruitment posters affect girls' career choices.

The day is divided into four two-hour periods, with a mid morning break at 10.15am., lunch at 12.45, and another break at 3.15 p.m. Usually two of these periods are taken up with radio theory and two with practical work, when we experiment with different radio circuits and also make various tools, such as spanners, screw drivers etc. We usually stop work at 5.30pm to be back at the depot in time for supper at 6.15pm, but on Mondays we stop an hour earlier and have about half an hour squad drill and on Wednesdays we have RT. and swimming. We are free after supper for the rest of the evening, but every Tuesday we have 'Canteen' when we get our chocolate ration and every Thursday we have the most important parade of all, pay parade. We are allowed to go out any evening but we must be in by 10pm except for two nights a week when we have late passes until half past ten. We may also go out for supper if we wish. 'Lights Out' is at 10.30pm and we are always ready for bed.

Every Tuesday and Saturday there are dances at the College, which are quite enjoyable. There are two or three cinemas within easy reach. As for sports, we can play tennis, swim, row, cycle or hike, just as we wish. We can also stay in and do our washing and ironing if we feel inclined - so we are never at a loss for anything to do'

Best wishes Yvonne Birch

Miss Stanton was still dealing with the problems arising from non-payment of fees. The problem was eventually solved with the implementation of the Butler Act of 1944 which introduced the eleven plus examination to select suitable youngsters to attend Grammar Schools and abolished school fees.

Like her predecessor, Miss Stanton sought to arrange a bus service from the bottom of the front drive into town, writing again and again to the Education Committee pointing out the difficulties the girls encountered walking to Leek to catch buses to outlying areas. The authority eventually agreed to fund the cost. (This facility was never extended to the pupils at the Boys' High School just 200 yards along the road from the bottom of Westwood Drive.)

In 1943 the caretaker retired and it was agreed by the governors that the sum of £5 should be paid to him for the existing crops and fruit trees in the garden. The advertisement for the post stated that he was to be responsible for the boilers, cleaning the buildings, taking care of the tennis courts, playing field and paddock. He was also to oversee simple repairs, reporting on the condition of the guttering, repairing the cold frames and glass houses and undertaking services as the head required. In spite of this list of daunting tasks, there were four applicants. Mr. J.Howson was appointed from 1st October 1943.

One very important change to the teaching staff followed the resignation of Miss Carless. She had come from the old Church High School as second mistress with Miss de Sausmarez and had acted as headmistress for one term. Her resignation was probably due in part to the new head's style of management. During only her second term in school Miss Stanton instituted an annual Parents' Day. Parents were invited to spend the afternoon in school to meet the new Headmistress and to be made aware of the activities available to all pupils.

Much to everyone's surprise Miss Stanton tendered her resignation to the school governors for 31st December 1945. She had been appointed as the headmistress at Newarke High School for Girls in Leicester. It is interesting to speculate why she stayed for only eight terms, a very short time for a head teacher. Did she find the pace of change, particularly related to staffing, too slow or was poor accommodation a difficult and frustrating issue? It was likely that the prospect of a new post in a larger, purpose built school with excellent facilities, was the main reason for her departure. The new school had opened in 1939 and had 600 pupils. In a letter written a few months after she left, printed in the school magazine, she compared the old and the new, Westwood and Newarke:

I often think of you all at this time of year, particularly of the trees and the gardens of Westwood. This school in many ways presents a great contrast. The buildings lack the beautiful exterior of Westwood but inside it is light and spacious and there are such luxuries as two gymnasia with showers and changing rooms adjoining. The hall has a beautiful platform, furniture, presented by the Old Girls Association and the hangings are in rich velvet. There are art rooms, domestic science rooms, and laboratories - all that a modern school should have.

This lack of facilities is often recognised by former pupils in their memories:

Janet Sellers 1945-50 (Mrs Wheeldon) relives some post-war memories.

As a youngster I attended St. Luke's Primary School at Endon. The war had just ended when I started at Westwood. I was fortunate to win one of the scholarships, but we had to pay for bus fares in those days. I remember it was 5d for a return ticket to travel to Leek and back each day. Even before I started at Westwood I felt that I had a connection with it, because my aunt had been a cook at the hall when the Johnson family had lived there. When the family left Westwood my aunt moved with them.

It was the end of the war and at first some of the girls wore panama hats in the summer, but gradually these were phased out because they were difficult to obtain. Some girls wore the green 'pork pie hats' but these were gradually replaced by the berets, possibly because not so much material was needed to make them. Our red and green ties were very narrow and may have had silk in them. They were made in the mills in Leek. After all these years I still have my school tie!

When I started at Westwood we had compulsory gardening lessons probably because the vegetables were used in the preparation of the school dinners.

Of course we all remember the characters on the staff. Miss Dugmore, our P.E. teacher used to roar up the front drive on her motor bike each morning. We jumped out of the way very quickly. I was in the hockey team and Miss Dugmore did a lot to help us. We didn't win many matches until she arrived and then she coached us and we were a lot more successful. We had a new games uniform consisting of navy shorts, white blouses and grey knee socks.

Miss Dugmore invited Mrs Paddy Dale, who was the goalkeeper for the All England Women's Hockey Team to visit the school. Everyone was so thrilled that such a distinguished visitor should come to encourage us with our hockey.

I remember Henry, who used to work in the school kitchens. He was a patient at Cheddleton Hospital. He was a lovely, friendly, young man, and he used to travel to Leek each day on the same bus as the girls. However, when the Mental Health Act came out he had to leave and return to life inside the hospital. Strangely enough I came across him years later when I was a nurse at the North Staffs Infirmary. Henry had been admitted because he had been very badly burned in an accident. Although he was suffering so much, I was very surprised when he spoke to me. He remembered me from the Westwood days.

A smiling group: Pat Thurlston, Nancy Myatt, Mary Taylor, Janet Sellers and Shirley Alcock.

Just before I left, the new canteen was opened. We were so pleased because it had been so difficult dining in the front hall. Sometimes some of the tables were set up in the narrow corridor that ran alongside the front hall. One advantage of being there was that we were able to leave quickly after dinner and race to the tennis courts to 'bag' them for a bit of practice.

I really enjoyed my days at Westwood and went on to do nursing, first at the Orthopaedic Hospital at Hartshill and then at the Infirmary.

Anne Mosley 1943-51 (Mrs Senior) recalls uniforms and home economics.

As a young girl I attended school at Kingsley and in 1943 I won a scholarship to Westwood. My first visit to the school was with my mother in the spring of 1943 when we met Miss Carless. I started at Westwood when Miss Stanton was beginning her second term as headmistress. Although I had won a scholarship place not all my expenses were covered.

At that time the uniform consisted of the usual gym slips with the box pleats. Girls who had older sisters who had attended the school wore the old style school hats which we called pork pies.' I wore a dark green beret purchased from Bayleys, the school outfitters in Derby Street, It cost my mother half a clothing coupon to buy it. In time something happened to my beret and I needed a new one. In those days we were able to buy new hats from Miss Ashworth at the stationery cupboard. (The old linen cupboard when the hall belonged to the Davenport and Johnson families). The new Beret never seemed to fit properly It always seemed to be too small. Sadly the second hat that I had had a very unfortunate accident. I was visiting some friends at Thornbury Hall near Cheadle and my beret landed in a static water tank. We fished it out but it seemed smaller than ever.

An essential piece of equipment was a shoe bag, hung on one's peg in the cloakroom. It contained indoor and outdoor shoes, and we had to change into suitable footwear. Coupons must have been a problem, and I imagine gym shoes were hard to come by. Substitutes were suggested. I remember the class being shown some that someone had made out of a car seat! (The District Nurse in our village obtained Wellingtons for my sister Kath and me through

Clothes rationing in the war years produced a variety of school uniform.

Dinner out of doors in 1946, accommodation in School was limited.

the Canadian Red Cross, and Miss Willis at the Sixth Form College told me about hers being mended with bicycle repair kits). At some stage we were asked to provide an overall to wear in the lab, and my mother made me one out of the lining of the blackout curtains. So it seems to be remarkable that when hockey shoes were required, I had a pukka pair from Daniel Meal's, the school outfitters in London! By post of course!

In Miss Greenstreet's needlework lessons we made nightdress cases, simple folded over envelopes with simple embroidery on them, and then we proceeded to the useless, shaped knickers, unbearable and a waste of clothing coupons.

My sister Valerie, eleven years behind me, had much more interesting cookery lessons than I did, but of course rationing had finished by then. For one lesson, the girls were asked to bring an egg. When they got to the point of using it, one girl found that she had mistakenly brought the hard boiled one put out for her father's packed lunch. We didn't hear what sort of a mess his raw one made.

One vivid memory that I have was of the distribution of milk at the school. It wasn't in bottles as it had been at the Primary School, but in a large bowl and one of the cooks scooped it out in a beaker. The milk had come from nearby Westwood Farm and I always felt it wasn't a very hygienic way of distributing it! One of the cooks, Mrs Hart, was responsible for administering first aid. She always stroked our cheeks and encouraged us to be brave.

After the war in 1945 there was a general election when Winston Churchill failed to be re-elected as prime Minister. We were discussing this fact at school and I declared that I was a Conservative. The girls I was with were horrified and pushed me to the ground and rolled me around to signify their disapproval.

Looking back I have been amazed that there was so little contact with our parents, beyond the occasional circular letter, bills for books and an informal sort of parents' day.

In the sixth form I was studying maths at advanced level. We didn't have the staff at Westwood to fully cover the subject and it was arranged with Mr. Ramsey, at the Boys' High school, for a group of us to join the boys there for lessons. Before we went Miss Bull had us in her study and stressed that it was polite to be on time for the lessons and on no account were we to be late. When we arrived at the boys' school, Mr. Ramsey called us into his study and asked us not to be early for the lessons, as he had nowhere to accommodate us. We were in a 'no win' situation!

It became a tradition to present the head girl with a medal and in 1951, as head girl, I was proud to be presented with the Provost Medal.

There seemed to be very few career openings for girls in those days. Most of the Westwood girls were advised to train as teachers or go into nursing. When I was doing the advanced level examinations my mother went to see Miss Bull and explained that I wished to go to university, but didn't wish to teach. She asked for her advice. Miss Bull suggested that I might like to be a Prime Minister's secretary. Apparently Miss Billington, who taught English on the staff, had held such a position before taking up teaching. As it happened when I finished at London University I went into industry, but then I lectured at the Technical College at Stoke and then at Madeley College: so I was teaching after all!

My mother had been a pupil at Westwood, then my sister Kathleen followed me and finally my youngest sister, Judith. My mother attended over twenty speech days altogether. I think this must have been a record!

Miss Taylor at the preparatory school.

Preparatory school pupils.

Chapter 6
The Preparatory School

Both the Girls' Church High School and Boys' High School had their own preparatory school from their beginnings in 1900. It was usually expected that the young children who attended the Preparatory School would after four of five years enter a form called Transition or Remove in readiness for entry into the High School at the age of ten or eleven. This type of education was usually limited to the children of middle class parents who could afford the fees. In the first two decades of the century the Prep.

The Nicholson Institute, with Greystones in front. The Preparatory School was to the right of the entrance behind the tree - see end of chapter.

School at the Nicholson Institute had its own headmistress and catered for boys and girls, whereas at the Maude Institute the Prep. Department was smaller and comprised mainly of girls.

With the reorganisation in 1921, the older girls moved to Westwood and all the young girls along with the young boys went to the one preparatory school in Stockwell Street. The one school would now feed the two high schools. Concern was expressed by Whitehall about the location of the new Prep. School being so close to the older boys. The arrangement lasted until 1939 when the Boys High School was transferred to the new buildings in Westwood Road, and from September 1939 the responsibility for the young pupils was transferred to the Girls' School. The Preparatory School pupils could now use some of the main Institute Building as well as the huts.

Gerald Mee a Prep. School Pupil 1933-39 remembers the start of World War II:

I first attended the school in about 1933/4 and went into Miss Rayner's Kindergarten class in one of the wooden huts, behind the Stockwell Street houses. This was a mixed class. I later moved to 'Transition' run by Miss Wildblood in the second wooden hut. This was prior to moving into form one in the main building. We had 'Ink Monitors' who had to go round the rooms filling up ink-wells in the desk tops. Very few of us stayed in school for lunch and most of us went home as it seemed the thing to do. We had the same uniform as the older boys. My parents bought mine from Baileys Sports outfitters in Stockwell Street, just opposite the school. Mr. Toby Warrington was headmaster until he retired and Mr. Ramsay took over in 1935. I was in 'Transition' at the time. In 1939 we moved down to the new high school, in Westwood Road, only to find that it was already occupied by boys from Burnage High School.They had been evacuated from Manchester. They didn't stay long, ironically, they went back to Manchester before the bombing had started there. When the young girls left 'Transition' they moved to Westwood, as the main school in Stockwell Street was for boys only.

The biggest change that parents would have noticed was in the new school uniform. It was now the red and green of the Girls' High School. Miss de Sausmarez took her new responsibility seriously, with frequent visits to the Prep. School. In 1948 the school, over a mile away at the Nicholson Institute, had only 12 girls left and Miss Bull wanted to integrate them into the main school, but the Education Authority in Stafford insisted they remain for another year.

Miss Taylor, who had been appointed to the Preparatory school in 1927 and had been in charge since 1939, moved to Westwood with the small group of girls in 1949. She was unsettled and quickly obtained a new post as headmistress at Shawell C. of E. School in Leicester.

Keith Davis a Prep. School Pupil, 1943-1945, touches on the 'make-do-and mend':

Many pupils were conveyed to and from school by their mum on a bicycle. Little seats, which clipped to the frame behind the saddle, could be purchased from the local cycle shop. It was wartime and there were not many private cars and petrol was unobtainable. I remember three members of staff, Miss Taylor of course, plus Miss Jensen and Miss Wildblood who supervised the transfer to secondary schools. Most of our classrooms were in the wooden huts to the right of the entrance gates, but there were some in the main building and if we entered here we had to change from our outdoor shoes to our pumps. All windows were taped over in a criss-cross pattern as protection against bomb blast. We also used the Carr gymnasium for special occasions. I remember singing my first solo from the platform, aged about six, in front of mums and aunts. (Dads were mostly at war) At breaks we played in the yard fronting what is now the college and there was access to a little kitchen round the right hand corner of the building facing on to the Carr gymnasium.

The door to the kitchen has long since disappeared. Milk was provided in mugs but was always too hot to drink in the time allowed. There was a star system as a reward for good work. There were all colours but it was the red, silver and gold that were most highly prized. A chart at the front of the classroom displayed pupils' progress or lack of it! We were usually given tasks to do in the holiday. Once we had to keep a weather chart entering 'cloudy', 'rainy' or 'cold' for each day of the holiday. A greater challenge was the requirement to construct a miniature garden in a small wooden box. I used a small face mirror for a garden pond.

One incident, which could have been tragic, concerned my cousin who somehow managed to get his head stuck in the very narrow gap between the Nicholson Institute gate pillar and the wall surrounding Greystones. He seemed to be there for hours weeping and wailing. The combined efforts of teachers, parents and pupils plus a butter lubricant finally freed him.

Her Majesty's Inspectors report of June 1951 opened by considering the preparatory department in Stockwell Street. They examined the history of the department under the Girls' School control. During the war years, it noted, its popularity had grown and numbers had almost doubled to 84 in September 1944. But as a consequences of the 1944 Education Act the Prep. School withered away, since no new entrants were allowed. Its final closure was in 1949.

Ruth Milner, a Prep. School Pupil 1944-1949 remembers its demise:

At the age of five years I travelled each day to the Prep. School in Leek from Cheddleton. It was lucky that I had adult company most of the way. I remember the school uniform with the green blazer and red badge which both the girls and the boys wore. Our three or four classrooms were situated inside the Nicholson Institute and not in the huts outside. School dinners were brought in from outside on trays. In winter the small bottles of milk were always frozen solid and had to be warmed on the heating pipes. I can only recall three subjects being taught: English, Maths and Nature Study, and we had use of the Carr gymnasium which was nearby. At the end when we were about to move to Westwood there were only about five of us left.

The end of the war and the impact of the 1944 Education Act was not lost on the girls, as the editorial in the 1946 school magazine shows.

1945 to 1946 was a year of change and transition. The world is adjusting itself often with surprising pain and difficulty, to peace, after a dreadful war. The working of the new Education Act has affected us, in common with every school in the country; we are appreciative of the great benefits in education which will come to all, but we cannot stifle some regrets at the passing of many things of the old order which were individual and personal

We have to watch our Preparatory Department disappearing and realise how much sadness and difficulty this is also causing to parents, (many of them old pupils of Westwood Hall and the Boys' High School) who wanted their children to have continuous Westwood Education from the age of five.

The Nicholson Institute. The Boys' High School and the Preparatory School were to the right of the Institute.

Miss Bull with the prefects 1952.
Back: Eileen Beaumont, Kathleen Morley, Anne Campbell, Christine Barber, Barbara Hall.
Sitting: Ann Shields, Ann Cundy, Miss F.M. Bull, Elizabeth Newton, Margaret Shatwell.

Some 6th formers 1956.
Back: Sheila Barrow, Jean Hodge, Joan Brocklehurst, Margaret Beard, Gwenyth Hine, Janet Dawson,
Seated: Anita Cliff, Ann Jackson, J. Johnson, Mary Harris, Lesley Bullock.

Chapter 7

Miss F.M. Bull, Headmistress January 1946-August 1955

Following the resignation of Miss Stanton, the post at Westwood was advertised and 45 applications were received. Miss Bull from King Edward VI High School for Girls, Birmingham, was appointed.

Florence Mildred Bull was the first child of Robert James Bull, a farmer on the Staffordshire/ Derbyshire border, and his wife Ida Mary. Florence was born in the late summer of 1908. She was educated at Uttoxeter Girls' High School and read English at Newnham College, Cambridge, where she was awarded her MA.

Her first teaching post was at Queen Elizabeth's School, Mansfield where she spent four years. Her next post was for ten years at King Edward VI School in Birmingham. She arrived at Westwood in January 1946 at the age of 37 years. At the same time, Mrs Hammersley was appointed as the new school secretary. Her efficiency and professionalism were to be a great benefit to the new head, and she became a well-known and much respected member of staff.

When Miss Bull arrived at the school the school uniform was in the process of being changed. The girls were still allowed to wear the old style navy uniform but now they also had the choice of wearing dark green gym slips. The blazers were dark green with the school badge emblazoned on the pockets in red and green. The school ties and scarves were red and green stripes. Coats could be navy or green. The white dresses for formal occasions introduced by Miss de Sausmarez had faded away and in the summer girls wore dresses or pinafore dresses in a mid-green material. The summer dresses were made to measure by Bayleys of Leek or by the girls' mothers. Doris Phillips remembers having this list sent to her in the spring of 1948.

WESTWOOD HALL GIRLS' HIGH SCHOOL, LEEK
REGULATIONS FOR SCHOOL UNIFORM

Hats	School beret with badge or
	Black hat (winter), Panama hat (summer) with school hat band.
	At present hats are not compulsory in the summer term.
School Blazers	The only alternative to a blazer is a plain dark blue cardigan.
Tunics	Winter - navy blue with knickers to match
	Summer - green gingham with knickers to match
	In the Summer Term, instead of a green tunic, a plain green cotton
	frock with white colour and cuffs may be worn.
	A navy skirt may be worn in the Sixth Form only.
Blouses	White or pale cream in winter blouses should have plain turned collar
	for wearing with a tie.
School Tie	
Stockings	White socks with summer uniform.
	Long brown stockings, or grey knee stockings, or fawn, grey or white
	socks in winter. An extra pair of socks or stockings should be kept in school
Shoes	A pair of indoor shoes (black or brown if possible) should be kept in school
Coat	A navy or dark green winter coat if possible
Hair ribbons	Should be black, navy, dark brown or green (plain)
	Slides should be plain brown.
	The School tie and hat band may be bought at School.
	Berets and blazers may be bought (with a permit from School) from Mr. Percy Bayley,
	Derby Street, Leek. Material for Summer Tunics and dresses may also be bought from Mr. Bayley

1948 SCHOOL PHOTOGRAPH

1948 SCHOOL PHOTOGRAPH

Miss Ashworth celebrated her 25 years of teaching in 1947 and donated a bible to mark the occasion. At the same time Miss de Sausmarez presented an oak table.

Miss Bull felt that some reminders of the war years needed to be tidied up and that the county architect should remove the air raid blast walls and the air raid shelters . The blast walls reduced the amount of artificial light in classrooms and the underground shelters were dangerous. These remains of the war were so carefully removed that pupils in later years could not work out where they had been. The grounds and estate had been restored to their former glory as one pupil remembers.

Joan Brocklehurst 1949-57 (Mrs Fleet)

Westwood was a beautiful country house with a long history, and its beauty, enjoyed on a daily basis, enhanced all our lives. For me, it was an opportunity to imagine life for the very rich, because

Miss Bull relaxes in the garden.

much of the rebuilt and extended house from the 19th century still existed in a relatively unaltered state; lead glazed and mullioned windows - some with internal shutters; well worn and polished original floors as well as magnificent quarry-tile floor, the immense wooded staircase in the front entrance / gym with its well worn treads and extremely shiny handrail; marble and stone fireplaces, and elaborate mouldings on the ceilings.

I would often sit in class or walk around school and dream about what the house had been like when families lived there instead of generations of school children. What we called the 'Front Hall' was particularly magnificent with its dark wood floors and panelled walls, lead glass windows, window casements and shutters and large stone fireplace.

There were many outbuildings around the main house, with stables and coach houses to the West that had been built in the late 19th century. The caretaker, Mr. Howson, and his family lived in this complex I remember carrying a very sick rabbit up the back drive during the myxomatosis crisis of 1953/55 to see if Mr. Howson, could do something for it. It was a bad time then and we were so upset to see all the rabbits suffering and dying at the sides of the back drive.

There were many wonderful and interesting plants in the grounds, such as abundant and mature azaleas lining the drive which created a vibrant display in the spring. I was particularly taken with a very large Cedar of Lebanon tree with its strange horizontal branches, located close to the front corner of the house. There was a pond at the side and large kitchen gardens behind the house with various greenhouses and cold frames close by. We would sometimes see the small indigenous red squirrels scampering around the grounds. What a magical place to go each day and to be surrounded by so much beauty and history.

The new Headmistress was well aware of the history of the school. She always enjoyed celebrating any occasion. In her first month at Westwood, during a period of national austerity, it happened to be the 25th anniversary of the founding of the school. Celebrations seemed to be in order and a tea party was arranged for the 27th September. The response to the new Headmistress's request to join in was tremendous. Those present included: the two previous headmistresses, Miss de Sausmarez and Miss Stanton, staff at the foundation of the school in 1921, the first Senior Mistress, Miss Carless, Mrs Pownall nee Bearpark and Miss Sant and the first head girl, Constance Arkcoll. There were governors, politicians and many old girls, two of whom made a grand entrance when they arrived on a motor bike! The cutting of the large tiered birthday cake was followed by short nostalgic speeches in which much was made of two words from the school motto, service and goodwill. There was much laughter and a few tears. All this took place on a beautiful autumn day. Miss Ashworth, who had joined the teaching staff in 1922, made a record of the occasion.

Westwood had always had an extensive garden. During the war years it had provided many of the vegetables used in the school kitchen. In the autumn of 1947 a new well-qualified gardener, Miss Tregorring, was appointed to teach gardening and to be responsible for the running of the kitchen garden. This appointment released Mr Howson to become a full time caretaker. He was

Miss H. Ashworth.   Miss E. F. Beck.   Miss Phillipson 1957.

Miss Bull and Miss Ashworth with the prefects in 1955.
Back row: June Messham, Avril Smith, Rosemary Lockett, Christina Brunt, Ruth Stabler.
Sitting: Janet Johnson, Jennifer Sheldon, Sheila Mayers Beryl Messham.

paid a £10 honorarium in recognition of his work in supplying the school kitchen.

Two years later, Miss Carder took over the part time post of Horticultural Instructress for two days a week. She made an immediate impact by creating a popular Friday Club activity which encouraged girls to get their hands dirty and write about their activities particularly in the school magazine. An article in the 1951 magazine explained the work of the Gardening Club:

Irene Kirkland and Bernice Johnson:

There are twenty two members in the gardening club this year, divided into four groups. One group looks after the rock garden. Later this year we hope to build the rocks up and to plant heather there, having a rock garden that will merge into the moorland. The second group looks after the herbaceous border and the third after the fruit. The last section sees to the weeds and looks after the vegetables and plants seeds. One of our members, Doreen Salt, arranged flowers throughout the school. During the winter we designed posters and discussed different aspects of gardening. Last year we visited Trentham Gardens to see the flower beds and such trees as the Swamp Cypress and a tulip tree.

Janet Dawson 1949-57 (Mrs. Hughes) also remembers the garden.

I have many happy memories of Westwood. In the Autumn I would go to school early, get off the bus and run up the drive to collect the conkers that had fallen from the trees onto the coke pile. I would often feed the squirrel who came at break for titbits. I enjoyed the delights of the kitchen garden, picking gooseberries and spinach, which was previously unknown to me, at the request of Miss Phillipson. The gym lessons were in a very small place in the entrance hall. We had very little equipment but they were still enjoyable (especially for a future PE teacher). I can recall doing 'long-fly' and ending up in the fireplace with Miss Gunnell. Also I remember getting outside to run round the games field to get fit. There was the difficult task of getting into our swimming costumes whilst on the bus heading for the town baths. When in the sixth form I was the first pupil to be awarded silver braid to edge my blazer, not as I initially thought for being good at games, but for not missing a match for a whole year.

As a country pupil, as opposed to a town pupil, much time was spent each day on bus journeys. Waiting for the ten past four Hanley bus outside the town centre cattle market was often enlivened by a visit to a very small sweet shop situated just by the bus stop where I could buy 'Milky Way' without sweet ration coupons. On Fridays and in wintry weather we would leave school early and at times we had to walk home as snow had stopped the buses.

Drama played an important part in school life with the annual form productions and competitions. For the joint productions with the Boys High School I remember helping to make cloaks.

As Head Girl, I had the privilege to accompany Miss Telford, the Headmistress, onto the stage for morning assembly. I also remember laying a wreath at Leek War Memorial on Armistice Day.

An inspection by county architects and officers concluded that significant changes needed to be made to the school. What is surprising is that it took so long, a quarter of a century, for the accommodation facilities at Westwood to be assessed as inadequate. The rooms used by the staff were badly congested and plans were drawn up to convert the attics on the west side of the school into staff rooms. Plans were also agreed for new tennis courts. The kitchens and their equipment in particular and were judged to be unhygienic and unsafe to use. New equipment and new cutlery were brought quickly into use.

Whereas the teaching staff was paid on the nationally agreed Burnham Scale, Kitchen Staff and cleaners were not paid well:

Cook Supervisor	£19.2.4 per month		
Cook (35 hours)	£ 2.13.51 per week	Gen. Assistant (35)	£2.10.5 per week
Part time Assistant	£ 1. 8. 9 per week	Cleaner	1s. 5 per hour

The spring term of 1948 brought the appointment of Miss Bell, from Ashbourne Grammar School, to teach scripture. She had an honours degree in English and a diploma in Theology from London University. Although an ample lady she was surprisingly light on her feet and loved to take girls for folk and country dancing.

Westwood was to have its first recorded burglary - it was Miss Bull's room and that of her Secretary that were the centre of attention. The head's room had been vandalised but nothing was missing. The secretary was distraught to discover the nearly £20 was missing from her drawer. A police investigation ensued. Pleas to Stafford for help were bluntly refused, the education authority pointing out that money should be banked promptly, not left in school and the school should carry its own insurance against theft.

Gwen Daykin remembers two sad incidents that could have ended more tragically:

One vivid memory I have was of a girl named Jean who had beautiful red hair. One day whilst we were conducting some science experiments with Bunsen burners, her hair caught fire. There were no cloths near her to throw over her, but someone had the sense to hit her over the head with an exercise book and succeeded in putting out the flames. It must have been traumatic for her. On another occasion when we were having swimming at those dreadful old Leek Baths, one of the girls almost drowned. She went down twice but fortunately a member of staff jumped in and succeeded in pulling her out, but she needed resuscitation before she recovered.

There was a keenness to involve parents more in school life so a tentative start was made with the formation of Westwood Parents' Guild to help in fundraising and to initiate social events. Subscriptions were set at a modest 2/6 per annum.

The Headmistress spoke with mothers of new girls each year making it plain what elements of sex education their daughters should beware of before starting school.

Miss Bull was keen to widen the curriculum encouraging pupils to go out into the world locally and nationally and by improving facilities for RE and games. Visits were arranged to many and varied venues including Norton Colliery, Wardle's Dye Works, a number of silk mills, the Gas Works by the station, the Sewage Works and Quick Fit and Quartz in Stone. Most of these visits took place out of school time usually on Saturday mornings.

Before visits took place parental and LEA permission was sought. Camping activities by the Girl Guide troop were encouraged as were overseas holidays organised by teaching staff. There were visits to Switzerland (cost £22.2s), Austria and Italy. The headmistress was aware that many pupils could not afford such holidays and applied for financial help, but she had little response. Trudy Wilcox 1949-56 (Mrs Blood) recalls a French trip, but not to France!

On another occasion my friend Anne and I went on a French course to a boarding school in Crawley, Sussex. Again it was a beautiful old house set in attractive grounds. However, we found it rather strange to sleep in dormitories and daunting when we could only speak French at meal times. We had to take it in turns to sit on the high table and chat with the staff.

One day the group planned to visit London. My friend and I said that we had already been and so we were left on our own for the day. We decided to take a bus to Bognor Regis and spend the day with a friend of ours who was on holiday there. When we returned, the group from London were just arriving back, so we simply joined the girls and no one appeared to have noticed.

Ruth Milner 1949-1957 remembers these visits vividly:

Miss Bull was very keen to encourage our appreciation of all forms of art and to widen our experiences. A number of visits were arranged to music concerts, dramatic productions, factories and businesses.

I particularly remember a visit we made to the Library theatre in Manchester to see' Oedipus Rex by Sophocles. When it reached the part where Oedipus blinded himself with one of his wife's brooches, one of our girls was so overcome she fainted. Yet more drama on this occasion!

Another visit was to Ludlow Castle to see 'Edward II' in the dramatic setting of the ancient castle. On the way we visited Stokesay Castle near to Craven Arms in Shropshire. It was a beautiful 13th century fortified manor house with a magnificent open hearthed great hall and a cruck built timber roof.

Visits to local pottery factories were memorable experiences too. We were fortunate to tour the Royal Doulton factory in Burslem, Wedgwood and Spode amongst others. These visits helped us to appreciate the skill of the potters as they transformed the balls of dull, grey clay into wonderful, brightly coloured works of art. Other visits were to Keele University to see a production of 'A Midsummer Night's Dream'. It was in the open air by the lake, a really magical setting. On another occasion we saw 'Romeo and Juliet' which was performed in the courtyard. These are such wonderful memories

For Trudy Wilcox 1949-56 (Mrs. Blood), the guide camp held fond memories:

At Westwood in the 1950s I belonged to the girl guides. We were the 4th Leek Company and we were really excited when our guide captain, Miss Griffiths, told us that we would be going to camp at Blackbrook, just outside Newcastle.

After the long bus journey from Leek we arrived at Blackbrook and settled into the bell tents that were already erected on the site. The camp was on a hillside and we were surrounded with tall pine and fir trees. The toilets were trenches that had been dug for us already and we just filled them in with soil a little at a time. We took turns to do the daily chores, preparing the vegetables, cooking meals and washing the utensils. I particularly hated peeling the potatoes.

During the evenings we would sit around the camp fire and as the flames leapt into the air we would sing our camp fire songs. We loved to sing, 'Ging, Gang, Gooli, Gooli, Gooli, Gooli, Watcha,' and 'Land of the silver birch, home of the beaver.' I liked the frightening ones such as the 'Witches in the graveyard'. For some of the guides it was the first time they had been away from home and they were very homesick sometimes, especially as it seemed to pour with rain nearly every day.

One afternoon Miss Harrison from Maer Hall invited the troop to visit her for tea. It was a beautiful old house similar to Westwood. There was a little bridge from the house to the church and the family would walk across it for the Sunday services. I remember the large hallway and being intrigued with the tiger skin on the floor, especially as its head was intact. Visitors came to see us and one afternoon my Auntie Nan Jones came and brought a cake for us to enjoy. Miss Caldicott, our R.E. teacher, also came and organised a treasure hunt for us.

Valerie Edwards put it all into a verse entitled simply 'Camp at Blackbrook':

Hurrah for the camp at Blackbrook, where
We spent our days in the open air;
Where the nights were short, and the days were long,
And our tasks were done with a smile and a song.
Hurrah for the Guiding games we played,
For the goods so fresh, and the eggs new laid!
How glad we were to see the camp,
When weary and worn, we returned from a tramp.
Hurrah for the camp-fire, burning bright,
That we fed with the fir cones, night by night,
And we sang as we watched the flames leap high,
While the sparks went whirling through the air.

Gwen Daykin 1949-56 (Mrs Giddings) also has vivid memories of the guides.

I have many happy memories of being in the Guides at Westwood. I was the patrol leader of the Chaffinches and I loved working for the many badges we could aim for. We once decided to camp at school for the weekend. I had to sleep on the floor with some other girls

Mary Harris, Gay Snow and Gwen Daykin at camp at Beaudesert.

in the bay windows of Miss Ashworth's form room. The floor was very hard and there were no curtains at the windows, so we woke up very early each morning when it got light. Miss Griffiths, our leader, slept across the corridor in the sickroom and so she was much more comfortable. Sometimes we cooked meals in the kitchens downstairs and at other times over camp fires in the wood.

A party visited the Festival of Britain on the South Bank site in London in May of 1951. All were well aware that the Festival was, in part, an attempt to raise spirits after a war and a long period of austerity. One girl wrote of her experiences:

During the day we explored the exhibition. First we went to see the 'Land of Britain' which included agricultural achievements. Then we visited a mine where machines demonstrated how coal was cut. Then after lunch we visited the Dome of Discovery. This included a section on the planets, a small weather forecasting station and an Antarctic section where there was a model of the type of hut used by polar explorers. We saw the type of food they ate and the sledges they used.

Only a few visited the Festival of Britain but all girls were given a commemorative silk bookmark designed and manufactured in Leek; many of these are still treasured.

Miss Bull was very concerned by the lack of sports, games and PE. facilities. Her predecessor, Miss Stanton, had written about the wonderful facilities at her new school in Leicester. This may have increased Miss Bull's determination to press for the building of a gymnasium, but in the post war period money and building materials were difficult to acquire. The area used as a gymnasium was most unsuitable. Often girls would run from the main corridor or the bottom of the stairs to vault the horse. Visitors to the school would occasionally have to negotiate a Gym lesson in full flow, having to pass though a class of girls in their vests and knickers. This was particularly off putting when boys from the High School came through for their Biology lessons! Full use was made of the existing tennis courts but a hard surfaced area was necessary. Plans were drawn up for new netball and tennis courts but it took five years of pleading to see the facilities constructed. In 1950 the opening of new courts was celebrated by inviting County players to hold exhibition matches.

Mavis Dale 1945-53 (Mrs Stanley) remembers the Spartan facilities.

I remember the problems with the gym and how low the ceilings were, so that when the girls did handstands off the box their feet almost touched the ceiling! There were no showers or proper changing rooms. We simply used the cloakrooms. When I left school I trained as a PE teacher! I

Leek Schools' Festival of Britain bookmark.

also thought it was strange that the staff rooms were in the attics but the staff cloakroom was on the ground floor. Another problem was that cookery was taught in a laboratory, equipped with one gas and one electric cooker for thirty of us. Another difficulty the staff had to overcome was to devise a timetable for 6 Ten (There were ten of us from the Upper

Hockey team 1949.

Back row:
Pat Lilley, Mary Taylor, Ann Ryan, Margaret Joy, Christine Dale, Janet Sellers.

Front Row:
Pat Wheeldon, Shirley Alcock, Margaret Hunt, Valerie Mayers, Pat Thurlston.

Hockey team in 1952.

Tennis team 1948.

5th who, having already done 5 years at the school, were too young to take GCE).

A friendship developed between the first headmistress Miss de Sausmarez and Miss Bull. There were invitations to visit the school, attend gatherings of former pupils and the final accolade, to sit for the painting of her portrait. On the Speech Day of 1950 the former headmistress presented prizes. At the request of the magazine editor Miss de Sausmarez described the changes that had taken place since her departure:

Mrs Mann with the netball team 1952.
Back: Ann Hulme, ?, Delilah Manning, Jean ?, Gladys Corden,
Front: Dinah Heaton, Mrs Mann, Helen Cope.

I have been asked to write about my visit in October. I will mention three outstanding events. First, school dinners in the new canteen! I could hardly believe it was there until I saw what a welcome addition it is to the school. You now have dinners in comfort, and the facilities in the kitchen and storeroom were never dreamed of by our kitchen staff. The only familiar thing was the noise.

Then in the evening the Old Girls' party in our former dining room where we were able to appreciate its spaciousness and the beauty of the panelling, and the log fire and the easy chairs and flowers added to its charm. There was a very representative gathering of old girls including many that were there at the opening of the school in 1921 and the photographs that Miss Ashworth collected caused much interest and amusement. I rejoice to know that the essential spirit of Westwood continues through the years.

September 1951 began with a nostalgic look backwards with celebrations to mark the 30th anniversary of the school's foundation. An elaborate thanksgiving service was organised at St. Edwards Church. Of the many guests and dignitaries, it was Miss de Sausmarez, who took pride of place. The service was conducted by the Vicar of Leek and a sermon was preached by the Bishop of Lichfield. The church was filled with pupils past and present, parents and friends.

In contrast, it was a very sad occasion when Miss Bull addressed a hastily called assembly on Wednesday the 6th February 1952, to inform all pupils that King George VI had died.

The news stunned all present and is an occasion remembered by many of those girls. It was in this hall in 1952 that the then headmistress, Miss Bull, sombrely greeted the surprised audience, which had no idea why it had been assembled, with the tearful words, 'The King is dead, long live the Queen.' We were all then immediately dismissed and sent home, to our great pleasure. (Joan Brocklehurst).

The following year the school celebrated the coronation of Queen Elizabeth. All pupils were given a coronation mug and 1s 3d towards a celebration tea by the Leek Urban District Council. On May 12th the school took part in the Coronation Music Festival and on the 28th a Coronation Party was held. It was a holiday from school on Tuesday 2nd June to celebrate the crowning. It allowed girls to follow the event on very small black and white television sets and join in one of the many street parties. A Coronation Carnival was held in Leek on the following Saturday when

School prefects 1952.

School prefects 1954.

Above:
'The Apple Cart' 1951
performed at Leek High
School.
Front: Audrey Beaton,
Margaret Walklett, Miss
Hill, Valerie Mayers and
Sheila Fallon.

'A Midsummer Night's
Dream' 1951.

CENTRE OF SCHOOL PHOTOGRAPH 1952. THE LEFT AND RIGHT SIDES OF THE PHOTOTOGRAPH ARE ON FOLLOWING PAGE.

the school produced a tableau for the procession depicting the Golden Hind. Much to the surprise of the school, celebrations were continued with a visit to the Grand Cinema in Leek to see a film of the Coronation and later 'The Conquest of Everest'. This visit was quite an event as it was the only time anyone could remember the whole school being taken to the cinema.

In this year Miss Bull supported by the Parents' Guild decided to commission a painting of Miss de Sausmarez from Mr. Bernard Dunstan. The work took nearly a year to complete.

In the autumn term of 1953 four new teachers joined the staff: Misses Mellor, Rice and Walker, the fourth member was male, the former High School Deputy Head, Mr. Price, who would teach Physics part time. Miss Mellor is remembered for building a canoe at the back of the laboratory and dissecting rats and earthworms to study their digestive and nervous systems. The smell of formaldehyde always seemed to be present in her laboratory.

Following the earlier success of *The Apple Cart*, another joint venture was undertaken by the two High Schools. The production of *The Mikado* was to have music, song and many more pupils. The bringing together of the pupils from both schools illustrated a shift in thinking about the contact between the sexes at school.

This first musical production proved to be a great success. Jennifer Sheldon, June Mesham and Glenys Powderhill played the three wards of Ko Ko (the High Executioner). Colin Wilson played the part of Nanki Poo and Rosalind Moorhouse was Katisha. Many of the individual performances were

outstanding and greatly appreciated by large audiences. The costumes and the fans filled the stage with colour. The pupils from both schools had helped with the costumes and the scenery. Two years later both schools joined together again to produce another Gilbert and Sullivan. *Iolanthe* proved another great success.

'The Mikado' 1954.

'Comus' 1955.

Anne Jackson 1948-56 (Mrs Biddulph) recalls these activities:

We had a school choir at Westwood conducted by Miss Wardill, and rehearsals always took place during dinner time. We would sing sometimes in assembly but the

'The Mikado' 1954.

'Comus' 1955.

highlight was singing for Speech Days, which were held at the Boys' High School.

There was also the inter-form dramatic competition, usually held during the spring term. Rehearsals would commence soon after Christmas, the plays being performed just before Easter. Form mistresses would help with the choice of the play, but rehearsals, costumes, props etc. were organised by the class who had voted to elect a producer. It was great fun. Taller girls were usually chosen for the 'male parts,' smaller ones had the more attractive roles! I remember our class being quite successful on a few occasions when the plays were judged. Sometimes we reached the finals and sometimes winning.

All performances were in the Back Hall as this was where we had the stage. It was very small and intimate, but when you reached the 6th form you were able to watch from the balcony.

Two highlights were the production of two Gilbert and Sullivan shows, jointly produced with the Boys' High School. Mikado - March 1954 and Iolanthe - March 1956 I'm sure that none of us who were involved in the Mikado had any previous knowledge of G & S, possibly never even heard of them. We were at last able to perform on a sizeable stage in a large hall!! It must have been a success as Iolanthe followed in 1956. Thus from these small beginnings, the Leekensian Amateur Operatic Society was formed. Miss Wrathall was a great support and eventually became president of the society. We had great experiences making costumes under the direction of Miss Martin and Miss Lakin.

I think I remember the Reading Competition. Each class, helped by the form mistress could choose either one or two entrants to represent the class again this took place in the back hall.

There was a great amount of mixed emotion: surprise, shock and amazement, when Miss Bull announced to a whole school assembly in the Summer Term of 1955 that she was leaving the school to get married. When Miss Bull tendered her resignation to the governors, they were glowing with praise for her work. She had been popular and respected by all.

'Iolanthe' 1956.

'Iolanthe' 1956.

'Iolanthe' 1956.

Joan Brocklehurst recalls her time at Westwood with fond memories:

Miss Bull, our headmistress for many years, was a very refined lady. I think that she often considered many of us to be country yokels. One day, in our first year, she objected to our Staffordshire pronunciation of her name, and we spent the whole class sounding out her name 'Bool, Bool, Miss Bool'. We still find it hilarious.

A very personal memory I have of Miss Bull in that very same year, is that she asked us to write one more verse to a poem that we had just read. I loved poetry and was always writing my own, and so enjoyed the assignment. When it was returned to us, I did not get mine back, and at the end of the class she asked me to accompany her to her room. Once there, she demanded to be told who had written my homework for me. I remember a great sinking feeling of helplessness and then considerable anger, as I insisted that it was I, and only I, who had done the work. I don't think that she ever believed me. She taught us English in the sixth form, concentrating on Gerard Manley Hopkin's poems. She did leave us with an enduring deep love of his "sprung rhythm" and themes of nature and religion.

On Friday afternoons we had clubs, one of which was the gardening club with Miss Carder, the biology teacher. We were let loose in the vegetable garden and spent many happy hours weeding, frolicking, falling and pushing over, and gardening in the sunshine. The library club for me was another great joy, as I could spend the whole afternoon browsing through the authors who were new to me. Always with a love for history, I spent many happy hours reading every book I could find by Geoffrey Trease.

Of the regular academic subjects, mention must be made of those teachers who did their best for us, some of them excellent in their pedagogy. Miss Griffiths was an excellent Maths teacher. She clearly taught us a new concept and then spent hours working through examples to consolidate the idea. Miss Beck taught Geography. Whilst at Westwood Miss Beck decided that as I was planning to read geography and geology at university I would benefit from some extra field work and she arranged for my friend Janet Dawson and me to go on local trips to check out the geography. Miss Ashworth drove their Morris Minor and we took off on Friday afternoons and mainly explored Cheshire, visiting picturesque churches on the way. We enjoyed science but our teacher probably didn't know the danger that we put ourselves in as we played with the beads of mercury that we had dumped into the slightly open drawers under the desk whilst half listening to the lesson.

Our scripture teacher was a stickler for the use of commas in our work. She would make us rewrite the sentences that we had not punctuated properly for our homework. It infuriated me so much that with one piece of work I put commas everywhere.

Some of our regular classes although not appreciated at the time taught life skills and left lasting impressions. Miss Martin's domestic science classes introduced us to making our own clothes - a pair of pyjamas - as we struggled with a variety of seams (French run and fell) a collar and shaped facings and button holes .In time her excellence as a teacher was recognised by pupils particularly those going on to careers in domestic science.

Each year, the whole school engaged in a 'dramatic Competition'. Preparing for it occupied many hours of our time. I was in most of the plays that we presented and we won in the Upper 5th with Wilde's play The Importance of Being Ernest. I played the part of Lady Bracknell wearing clothes that had belonged to Freda Harrison's grandmother.

'The Importance of Being Earnest' 1952.
Back: Sheila Barrow, Wendy Barber, Joan Brocklehurst, Gillian Frost, Marlene Belfield.
Front: Mavis Mellor and Edna Bloor.

Miss Beck and Miss Ashworth were very kind and considerate and this is reflected by Trudy Wilcox:

On one memorable occasion my friend Anne and I went to spend the night with Miss Beck and Miss Ashworth at their home in Nab Hill Avenue. We had been asked if we would like to see a production of The Pied Piper in Leek. We explained that it was difficult for us due to problems getting back home late at night. My father offered to pick us up but at the last minute he had to attend a meeting, so Miss Beck and Miss Ashworth offered to put us up for the night. Consequently after the production they drove us to their house in their car.

Anne went to bed early as she had a geography exam the next day. As Miss Beck was her geography teacher she was planning to do a spot of revising under the bed clothes with her torch. I stayed up longer and our two teachers seemed to ask a lot of questions about my family. The following morning at breakfast, their cat made a surprise jump to land on Anne's lap. Anne half fell off her chair and her toast shot across the table straight just missing Miss Beck's plate.

Having left school at the end of the Summer term Miss Bull married the Revd Albert Hearn of Hale in Cheshire. Miss Ashworth also retired at the end of the summer term having served the school for 33 years, almost the entire life of the school. Presentations were made to both retiring teachers at the end of term.

Miss Bull had left Westwood in July and the time of her resignation did not give sufficient time for a permanent replacement to be appointed for the start of the new school year so Miss Beck was appointed acting headmistress for the autumn term of 1955. At the Speech Day in that term Miss Bull (now Mrs Hearn) was invited back to present the prizes. In her address she thanked everyone for their help and loyalty. She contrasted her new home in the city suburbs with the beautiful surroundings of the school at Westwood. Following her retirement, Mrs Hearn (Miss Bull) wrote for the school magazine about her life, present and past:

> *For some weeks after I stopped coming to School I was frequently conscious of my timetable alongside my simpler one of housekeeping and I lived, as the Shakespearean critics might say, in 'double time'. As I scurried on with the washing-up and cooking and gardening I would wonder if the Lower Fourths were having games and gardening, or the Upper Fifths Latin and Domestic Science, or if 6A would be reading Gerard Manley Hopkins. Lately, I have thought of you more in changes of the weather and indeed the sun shining on your azaleas or through the great beech tree, or wondering if the foxgloves were out yet in the wood, or if the rain had kept you indoors at break*
>
> *I have been delighted to hear of your recent successes and I am glad to have the opportunity to send my very best wishes to the school and to each of you. It is good to think that wherever we are we share the same Westwood motto: 'With Good Will Doing Service.'*

It is not surprising to note that most memories of this era are not of lessons and examinations but of sights, surroundings, incidents and adventures with friends.

Anne Bainbridge 1949-1956 (Mrs Lewis):

When I think of my first day at school many vivid memories come to mind, even though over half a century has gone by. There was a mile and a half walk to Baddeley Green, from my home at Light Oaks, followed by a long bus journey on a crowded double-decker bus to the bottom of Ladderedge. Here I found myself at the bottom of a long, winding, gravel drive that meandered through lush, green fields. I followed the trail of girls, all wearing green and navy, complete with little green berets, and satchels over their shoulders. We went past the bushes thick with shiny black elderberries, past the sticky bud bushes and the rabbit warrens. The drive appeared to have no ending, but by a lodge at the top we went through a wide gateway and I caught my very first sight of my new school. It was a large, stately house, complete with a clock tower and tennis courts. At the side of the courts on the west front was a beautiful summer house with a gothic type doorway and constructed from the same warm coloured sandstone as the main house.

We were shown to the cloakrooms in the main kitchen area and hung our pump bags on the pegs allocated to us. Then we changed our outdoor shoes for lighter indoor shoes, a ritual we would carry out every school day for the next seven years.

Our classroom was situated on the upper floor, towards the back of the building, and it was pleasant and airy. When I lifted the lid of my desk at break I still remember the smell of the toast my mother had packed for the mid-morning snack. As I was away from home from 7.30am until 5pm each day she seemed to think that I would starve! The French homework that first day was an essay on, 'Why do I want to learn French?'

We soon fell into the daily routine, gathering in the front hall each morning to sing, one of a small selection of hymns 'Morning has broken,' and 'Breathe on me breath of God.' were two favourites, but on Friday mornings we always sang,'God be in my head, and in my understanding.'

We had order marks if we were in trouble, and two order marks resulted in a detention, when we had to remain in school Friday afternoons and do extra work.

During my seven years I received just two detentions, the first was given in a Cookery lesson. I was fooling around with a friend shaking the flour dredger at her. Unfortunately the top came off and she was covered in flour! My second came for not doing my home work. We were told to make a model of an African village but I decided not to. What was not appreciated by teachers was that I had to walk over a mile to catch a crowded bus into Leek and then walk up the drive. The rain and wind helped to convince me that I would never get the model to school in one piece.

We were expected to keep our form rooms very tidy and we competed for the tidiness bowl each week. We always stood up when a teacher entered the formroom. Collections for various charities were also made weekly. If we walked with very straight backs we were awarded deportment girdles of red and green. These were tartan type sashes worn in place of the normal belts or girdles. Of course it helped if we were born with lovely, straight backs!

I loved to explore the grounds surrounding the school. The disused pond with the forgotten water features fascinated me, together with the miniature garden that some of the girls had constructed in a large wooden seed box at the bottom of the tennis court steps. The wood at the top end of the playing field was full of sweet chestnut and beech trees. Red squirrels scurried along their branches and the rhododendrons formed quite a thick undergrowth. When the leaves started to fall in the autumn we would try to catch them before they reached the ground, because they would bring good luck and we could make a wish.

One vivid memory I have happened in one of our biology lessons. Some of the boys from the Boys' High School used to join us for these sessions. Miss Mellor, our teacher, was dissecting a

Lower IV July 1947.
Left to right: M. Simpson, M. Dale, M. Ferneyhough, J. Knight, F. Edwards, A. Rex, B. Clement, D. Smith, B. Hall, B. Ash, E. Robinson, M. Mears, D. Heath, D. Brough, P. Lisle, T. Bettany, P. Graham, J. Cope, J. Horley, Mrs Mann, G. Harris, S. Braddock, J. Sims, M. Taylor, A .Shields, J. Titterton, B. Rhodes, D. Brown, D, Phillips, K. Lovatt, P. Lilley, M. Morris, M. Brew, H. Moores, B. Bowcock.

Upper 4A 1952.

Back:
Mavis Mellor, Dorothy Hall,
Elaine Baggaley, Sheila Barrow,
Josephine Rushton, Mary Bass.

3rd row:
Margaret Stubbs, Marcia Stubbs,
Janet Warrington, Trudy Wilcox,
Marion Jackson, Anne Bainbridge.

2nd row:
Pat Kent, Phyllis Brew, Gillian Frost,
Edna Bloor, Jean Clulow.

Front row:
Valerie Edwards, Mary Harris,
Elaine Shenton, Nora Richards,
Barbara Johnson, Anita Cliff,
Norma Sharpe, Lesley Bullock.

mouse and we were really concentrating on the procedure when one of the boys suddenly fainted and hit the ground with quite a bump. He wasn't hurt and soon recovered but of course the girls found this quite amusing.

At Christmas there were parties to enjoy. We were allowed to bring special party dresses to change into. After Christmas there were the dramatic competitions, when lessons were suspended and we had an idyllic time watching one play after another. At the end the adjudicator would do the summing up and the prize would be awarded. In due course the reading competitions were held and marks were awarded for diction, pronunciation, expression and delivery. The tennis tournament took place at the height of summer and finally just before the summer holidays commenced, the school magazine was published. Then after what seemed a long year the school gathered together for the final service before the holidays. We sang the school song, and many girls wept as we also sang, 'Lord dismiss us with thy blessing, all who here will meet no more.' But there was a much happier side, at last the holidays had begun

Enid Partington 1953-60 (Mrs.Ball)

Even as young girls we appreciated the need of school rules for the good of us all, but sometimes there seemed to be so many and some seemed so unnecessary.

Uniform had to be worn at school and the beret was essential when travelling to and from school. There was no running in the corridors and we always had to keep to the left hand side of the corridors and staircases.

Certain areas of the school were out of bounds; the clock tower, the cellars, the attics, except when asked to visit the dramatic cupboard to collect costumes for the plays, or to pick up sets of books stored there.

Pupils travelling to school by bicycle always had to walk with their bicycles up and down the drive, except at dinner times when time was short before they had to return to school, and also there were not so many people about. The girls were not allowed to eat when walking along the streets and if they were caught they would be reported by a prefect.

Of course school rules were sometimes broken. I recall the day when I had been playing in the wood with some of my friends. I think we had been building dens in the rhododendron bushes. One of our group decided that it would be fun to climb over the gate at the end of the wood and explore the fields beyond, which of course were out of bounds. We all agreed to the idea and enjoyed investigating the mysteries beyond the gate. We didn't hear the school bell from where we were and after a while we decided that it must have been time to return to school for the afternoon session. So we scrambled over the gate, hoping that we weren't too late. In our haste one of my friends fell and broke her arm. We managed to help her back to school and get help for her. Questions were asked about where we had been, what we were doing, and how the accident had happened. Of course we had to explain everything and we were in very serious trouble.

Other girls would explore the building, often risking life and limb in doing so. These two incidents were told to the authors. A group of girls walking out of school late one evening, having stayed for prep, noticed a ladder propped up the side of a tower window. As the coast was clear the opportunity to climb was too tempting. Inside the tower they found a small room with part of the floor missing looking down they could see the floor in the back hall far below! On another occasion the same group of girls decided to explore the attics. They moved from one small room to another until they came to a locked door and peered through the key hole. To their amazement they discovered that it was one of the staff rooms!

Miss June Wrathall (teacher 1954-1981) recalls her first impressions:

1954 was the year I decided to spread my wings and apply for a Head of Department post. There were two posts advertised which caught my interest: one in Richmond, North Yorkshire, and one in Leek, North Staffordshire. Richmond proved impossible as I would have had to teach Needlework to fill my timetable, so I did wonder what the catch would be in the Leek post, which was also a small school.

I travelled by bus to Leek. I was told to get off at the Monument, where a taxi would be waiting to take me to Westwood Hall Girls' High school. I was a bit puzzled when the Monument turned out to be a clock tower, I had expected a statue of some Leekensian dignitary and the taxi looked as though it was from the 1930's. We travelled at a dignified pace out of Leek and eventually turned left into a lane by the lodge. I really did wonder if it was the right road, but my driver was not given to talk and ignored my rather anxious queries. It was with some relief that we eventually turned into the grounds of what looked like a very respectable country house - but surely not a school? What a relief when I opened the front door and heard a bell ring, doors opening, girls and teachers suddenly emerging - all the normal sounds of a school. I was taken to the office and then to the staffroom. It was another surprise to discover the staffroom was in three consecutive attics! Then I was promptly cross examined by Miss Lakin, who expressed surprise that there was a University at Manchester I was not sure whether she was serious or joking.

Then Miss Ashworth and Miss Beck took over, offered me tea or coffee and made me feel welcome. The rest is history. The country house really was Westwood Hall, High School.

Guides at Blackbrook 1952. Mrs Griffiths, Guide Leader, is seen bottom right.

Enjoying the sunshine 1955. ? Janet Dawson, June Mountford & Gwenyth Hine.

VI Ten in July 1951 - too young to take the G.C.E. exams.

Standing:
Barbara Hall, Gwen Harris, Christine Barber, Miss K.M. Bell, Margaret Brew, June Hambleton, Kathleen Mosley.

Kneeling:
Joyce Cope, Barbara Ash, Barbara Bowcock, Mavis Dale.

Upper 4 R 1952.

Upper 4 R 1952.

Chapter 8
The 1951 School Inspection

A formal inspection was conducted by His Majesty's Inspectors in June 1951, only the second in the history of the school and 18 years after the first. The inspectors' report was full of facts and figures, observations and assessments made coolly and calmly by people well versed in looking at schools. It highlighted the fact that at the end of the War Westwood had had 357 pupils, the largest number in its 30 year history. This figure excluded the preparatory department. During the next five years a move to reduce the serious overcrowding meant that at the time of the inspection the number was 295.

An analysis of the location of the girls' homes revealed that 50% lived in Leek and 50% in the surrounding area. The fact that many pupils were bussed into school dictated the time set for the end of the school day and limited the participation in after school activities to a certain extent.

An analysis of the destination of girls leaving the school in the three years prior to the inspection showed an interesting pattern, one that was to be familiar throughout the school's subsequent history. Of the 201 girls who left, only 25% had been in the sixth form. Eight went to university, 30 to teacher training colleges, 14 to nursing and 34 to other schools. The girls had very little career advice as the teaching staff had little knowledge of the world of employment outside education.

The inspectors were admirers of the setting of the school noting that it was such a delightful place to be educated in. *The school stands in beautiful surroundings and the condition of the lawns, flower beds and most of the woodland is admirable.*

A view of the Hall greatly appreciated by the Inspectors

They did note that the 650 yard drive from Westwood Road up to the school entrance was full of pot holes. The unsuitability of the accommodation was highlighted as was the very slow rate of progress in adapting the buildings and the grounds. The issues were very simple. The school building had too many small rooms, often unsuitable in shape and many lacking sufficient natural light. The new kitchen and dining room were of temporary constructions. The conversion of the attics in the roof into attractive staff rooms was the only real success.

In the eighteen years between the two inspections there had been only slight improvement to the playing fields. New tennis courts were laid in 1949, but there was still a pressing need for a gymnasium. It is interesting to note that though the inspectors were fully aware of the deficiencies in classroom and specialist accommodation, few of the ex pupils who shared their memories, mentioned the concerns highlighted.

The section on the staff was far from complimentary. There was the equivalent of 16 full time teachers, made up of 13 full-time, 4 part-time, plus a teacher from the Boy's High school. This number of staff was not ungenerous. The inspector pulled no punches in their assessment of the staff in the final paragraph:-

The staff representing as it does a diversity of age and experience is well balanced but qualifications are only mediocre. With exception, the teaching heard was dull. Not enough was demanded from older girls; girls were not made to speak up and frame proper replies or encouraged to initiate discussions.

Criticism was made about the lack of grading (setting or streaming) in the first four years. It was only in the fifth year that mixed ability was set aside. The lack of streaming on ability grounds was seen as the major factor in poor performance, particularly in Latin and Mathematics. Their criticism was more robust in the report:

The work of the school is on the whole of only moderate quality; Music and Religious Instruction were comparatively strong subjects; Latin and Science comparatively weak. Difficulties of accommodation have handicapped Physical Education and Art.

In their final analysis H.M.Is identified three areas where change was necessary if academic standards were to improve:

1. Improvements to school buildings were essential. This change was to take about two more decades to accomplish.

2. Recruitment of high calibre staff was a priority. Here the inspectors were assuming that high academic attainment at university produced high calibre teachers. This assumption was, and is, not necessarily true.

3. The new GCE examinations would help pupils and teachers to pursue their strengths and interests. What the inspectors did not mention was that the percentage mark needed for a pass in a subject was significantly increased.

The inspectors admitted that education was not all about academic achievement when they stated: *There is a family spirit about this school and the manners and appearance of the girls made a favourable impression on the inspectors.*

The staff was relieved when the rigorous four day inspection was over. Most staff must have felt disappointed when the report was published and its contents and findings discussed. This, most likely, once in a life time scrutiny of their professional competence and ability, would have left its mark. In the new school year, Miss Bull had the task of lifting staff moral and carrying the school forward. Few pupils were aware of the importance of the inspectors visit even though one did remember having a lesson outside on the lawn so that the teacher could avoid a formal assessment.

SCHOOL PREFECTS, 1949—1950

Head Girl—Dorothea Nixon

Deputy Head Girl—Margaret Joy

H. Mary Boulton	Winifred M. Jordan
E. Christine Dale	Anne Mosley
Mary Deakin	Brenda Newbon
Margaret A. Fern	Stella M. Parrack
Margaret M. Hunt	Patricia M. Wheeldon

SCHOOL CALENDAR, 1949—1950

Autumn Term

Sept. 6—Term began. We welcomed Miss Martin and Miss Gunnell as new members of staff, also Miss Taylor and five remaining members of the Kindergarten in Stockwell Street.

" 26—School Holiday

" 27—The School's Birthday   an exhibition of tennis by four County players.

Oct. 7—Party to see the Lanchester Marionettes at the Carr Gymnasium, Leek.

Nov. 2—Visit of Mrs. Dale, England Ladies' Hockey Team goalkeeper

" 4 & 7—Half-Term Holidays.

" 11—Speech Day. Prizes distributed by Dr. Smith, headmistress of King Edward's High School for Girls, Birmingham.

" 14—Lecture by Mr de Witt Batty, Archdeacon of Ahmednagar, with the VIth form of Leek High School. Lecture to the middle school about a Home and School for Blind Children in Persia, by Miss Oaster.

" 21—Speech Day Holiday

Dec. 13—Junior Christmas Party.

" 14—Middle School Christmas Party.

" 15—Talk by Rev. N W Watson, Vicar of Leek, illustrated by lantern slides.

Upper V form's Christmas Party.

" 19—Sixth Form's Christmas party at Leek High School.

" 20—Junior carol service in the morning, senior in the afternoon

" 21—End of Term. We said goodbye to Miss Billinton, Miss Ogilvy, and Miss Taylor.

Spring Term

Jan. 10—Term began. We welcomed Miss Lakin and Miss Watson to the Staff, and Mrs. Turner who is a former member

Feb. 23-27—Half-Term Holiday

Mar 1—Road Safety Quiz for girls under 15 years.

" 6—Road Safety Quiz between a Westwood team and a team at Endon Secondary Modern School. Westwood won 66-63 points.

Mar 14—A Westwood team beat a Leek High School team in a Road Safety Quiz.

" 15-16—A party went to Longton to see *The Servant of Two Masters*.

Presentations of plays in the Dramatic Competition.

" 22—The finals of the Dramatic Competition, won by Form Lower IVs.

" 24—An S.C.M. meeting in Newcastle addressed by Lord Lindsay of Birker, speaking on "Christianity and Communism."

" 27—A party went to a World Youth Forum in Manchester, the subject, "My Country and World Peace."

" 28—A play reading of *The Importance of Being Earnest* by Oscar Wilde.

" 29—Staff v 1st XI hockey match. The school won, 7-0 goals.

" 21—A Westwood team was beaten by the East Street School team in a Road Safety Quiz.

Senior Netball Final, won by Form Lower V b.

" 30—Junior Netball Final, won by Form Upper IV a.

" 31—Senior Hockey Final, won by Form VI.

April 3—A Jubilee presentation to Leek High School.

" 4—The Seniors visited the Arts and Crafts Exhibition at Leek High School.

" 5—End of Term. We said goodbye to Miss Sharples and Miss Watson.

Summer Term

April 26—Term began. We welcomed Miss Machin, and Miss Knight as a former member, to the Staff. We used the school canteen for the first time.

" 28—A party to see *Macbeth* in Newcastle.

May 6—A party to see *Julius Caesar* in Stratford-on-Avon.

" 8—Senior Gymnastic Competition.

" 9—Junior Gymnastic Competition.

" 14—A party to see scenes from *Henry V* in Leek.

" 29-June 2—Half-Term Holiday

June 15—A party to see a French film show in Leek.

" 16—Lecture to VI a by Mr Vinen on "Books and Libraries," in Leek.

" 21—Junior School Parents' Afternoon.

" 22—Middle School Parents' Afternoon.

July 20—Senior School Parents' Afternoon.

" 28—End of Term. We said goodbye to Miss Swainson.

NORTHERN UNIVERSITIES JOINT BOARD 1949
HIGHER SCHOOL CERTIFICATES

H. Mary Boulton—Good in French, Pass in English Literature, Latin and Subsidiary History

Chapter 9
The School Magazine

The School Magazine is an important source of information about the school and its numerous activities. It was usually edited by a sixth former supported by two assistants and there was teaching staff supervision. In the first two decades of the 20th century, Leek Church Girls' High School had a very finely produced magazine. It was called *The Orange and Black,* and was produced termly. The quality of the literary content, and its production in terms of print and paper was never to be matched. The 'Westwood' Magazine was first produced in 1925 and annually thereafter. A tradition was established that was to last for four decades. Parts of the editorial in this first edition are worthy of note as they record the early and tentative steps.

Westwood is now nearly four years old, and it is well that at least some of her doings should be placed on record. We do not want our Magazine to be merely a chronicle of events; we want it to be indicative of the spirit of the school. I think very few of us realize that as the first members of a new school we have a tremendous responsibility. It is for us to lay the foundations that others will build upon. We must remember that any school traditions that may owe their origin to our efforts will remain and be part of the School, long after we have left it. Good beginnings count for so much.

The magazine never had a name and the cover was usually green, the shade varying from very light to very dark. There was an exception in 1928 when the cover was brown and the recently adopted School motto had pride of place, at the front. The following year a competition

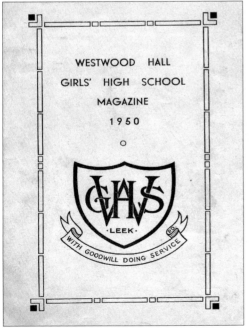

Magazine Cover. Note the initials P.D.

was held to produce a design for the front cover to replace the very small flower motif. Only four entries were submitted and that from Peggy Davies was selected as having the simplest design and most careful workmanship. Her design appeared on magazines from 1929 onwards, it was a shield with the 5 letters WHGHS in cipher form and also included on the shield was the word 'LEEK'. The school motto and the initials PD were written on the scroll below the shield.

The magazine was initially 18 pages long and eventually reached 28 pages. In the 1930s it changed its size to quarto and was printed in house. There was no magazine published in the early war years 1939-42 but one of Miss Stanton's early initiatives was to commence publication again in 1943. For many years it did not contain any photographs, but in the late 1940s there was occasionally one of the head girl, or one of the staff on a separately inserted sheet. Photographs appeared with the text in the 1950s

Jean Bratt's photograph
- one of the first to be included
in the magazine.

usually showing sports teams or the prefects with the headmistress.

Much in the magazine was, by its very nature repetitive, with its detailed school calendar for the year usually compiled in retrospect. There were staff appointments and departures, examination successes, Speech Day reports, games results, developments in the library, pieces of poetry, records of visits, an occasional piece from the Preparatory Department, letters from old girls and on the back pages records of marriages and births and very occasionally deaths. A successful formula was developed. The editors often had a difficult task in getting original work for the magazine so in the 1920s and 1930s a clock was awarded to the form submitting most material. The early editions had a number of themes which were followed and developed. Additions to the library were listed individually. This did fill half a page! Poems took up 3 or 4 more pages but the highlight was the hockey first 11 team reports and individual player evaluation which showed sports' journalism at its best. Two examples give the flavour:

Left Wing-Kathleen Hammond. Kathleen has improved very much, but is apt to be selfish. An opportunity for shooting is often lost by not passing in at the 25 yard line, but on the whole she is good and reliable' She was awarded her colours.
Left Half-Joan Whittles. Joan is good on the whole, and would be very good if she was quicker on the ball and had more control over her feet. She was not awarded her colours.

The Old Girls' Association usually had a report included, but seldom were they as high brow raising as the entry in the 1944 issue, where it was recorded that a very successful dance was held in the Town Hall in Leek to which 50 members of the U.S. Forces were invited.

The editorial in the first magazine published after the war (July 1945), showed that pupils were aware of the significance of those years as well as the debt they owed to others and the contribution they could make in a post war world:

Since the last publication of our magazine, we have watched with our Town, our Country and the world, the mighty climax of this war and the coming of peace to Europe. In view of these great events we put forward this record of an ordinary school year with utmost humbleness, knowing that our success and failures rank low beside the great achievements of our time.

Yet we must not feel that our interests and actions are apart from the stream of national life and world events. Wars in the past were remote from the life of the ordinary man and woman, but we have just seen the end of a citizen's war. School must never forget that some of our most skilled and valiant soldiers, sailors and airman came from schools such as we have here in Leek. Girls who, six years ago, and more recently than that, were immersed in Geometry, Grammar and Games have gone all over the world in the Women's services to fight, to cook, to nurse, while others stayed at home to serve as housewives, gardeners and factory workers.

Some of you may feel that with the end of the war your great chance of service has passed, but that is not so. Victory has been given *to us. Peace must be of our making. In small ways it is in the hands of us all, if this victory number of the Magazine includes some indications of how you may work for others, it will have justified its production.*

The winter of 1946-47 allowed the editor to consider the happier side of very harsh weather when many girls outside the town could not get to school:-

Most of the time from Christmas to Easter, the countryside lay under deep snow and frost. If it was a daily polar expedition to Westwood, we did have all the fun of the drifts, the pallid beauty of the winter scenes to appreciate, and a log fire in the entrance hall.'

There was often unintended hidden humour in the writing. The editor in 1948 was appreciative of changes in the School's limited accommodation, but did she really mean to express it this way?

Two additional rooms were made available for use as form rooms when the staff left their first-floor staff rooms and generously ascended to the attics.

The school year calendar for 1949-50 lists over 40 events, but recorded nothing of lessons. The calendar's first entry of September 6th noted the arrival of new members of staff - Miss Martin and Miss Gummel. One of the last recorded the departure of Miss Swainson. But almost hidden in this entry was the arrival of Miss Taylor and the five remaining pupils from the Kindergarten in Stockwell Street. The Preparatory School had finally been closed in the previous July a point missed by most people.

Each magazine had its editorial and these provide astute observation of school life. 1953 was the Coronation Year, a very

all who took part. The School won at netball but the Old Girls beat the School Eleven at hockey We hope to play a tennis match against the School in July.

We should like to invite all Old Girls to join the Association, the membership fee being 2/6, payable in January each year Send your name to the Secretary —Miss S. Morrow, 29, Haregate road, Leek.   B. NEWBON

NEWS OF OLD GIRLS

Dinah Heaton won the Gold Medal at the North Staffordshire Royal Infirmary

MARRIAGES

Taylor—Birch. On August 28th, 1954, at S. Edward's Church, Leek, Raymond B Taylor to Mona Birch.

Bayley—Wheeldon. On August 19th, 1954, at Mount Methodist Church, Leek, Michael H. Bayley to Patricia M. Wheeldon.

Thacker—Ratcliffe. On July 12th, 1954, at S. Chad's Church, Longsdon, Alan Thacker to Elvin Ratcliffe.

Kenway—Clarke. On July 10th, 1954, at S. Luke's Church, Leek, Frank W Kenway to Mavis Clarke.

Yates—Ashley On July 24th, 1954, Anthony Yates to Shirley Ashley

Scrivener—Hazlehurst. On August 12th, 1954, at S. Edward's Church, Leek, Brian H Scrivener to Shirley Hazlehurst.

Palmer—Stanley On December 27th, 1954, at Blandford, Dorset, Gordon Palmer to Alma Stanley

Llewellyn—Chadwick. On 19th February, 1955, at S. Luke's Church, Onecote, John Llewellyn to Olive Chadwick.

Brassington—Cantrill. On April 23rd, 1955, at Rushton Methodist Church, John Brassington to Elizabeth Cantrill.

Bourne—Tunnicliffe. On May 7th, 1955, at S. Luke's Church, Leek, Dennis Bourne to Joan Tunnicliffe.

Blackwell—Bailey On May 21st, 1955, at Ipstones Parish Church, Leon J Blackwell to Jessie Bailey'

BIRTHS

Haime.—On May 12th, 1955, to Beryl (née Tipper), wife of Douglas Haime, a son, Philip John.

Harris.—On June 10th, 1955, to Paula (née Peacock), wife of F Harris, a son, Richard Michael Colin.

special time. Every girl had a coronation mug, a gift from the Council, a party and a chance to take part in the town's carnival. In this eventful year, the editor expressed eloquently the essence of the School and the purpose of the magazine.

> Although the year has been unique, Westwood is essentially the same as when it was founded over thirty years ago; it is still a community of happy girls enjoying the varied advantages of the school. We hope that through the magazine some of the spirit and character of Westwood will be revealed.

Sylvia Mellor then in 3E, writes about a special party to celebrate the Coronation:

> Our Coronation party was on May 28th . We had an early dinner and then we changed into party dresses. Soon after 2pm the party started. We went onto the paddock for a treasure hunt. On a

The coronation mug presented to all pupils in Leek.

> blackboard was a jumbled word. After finding out what it was we could start off. The word was 'doormat' so we set off looking under all the doormats. We searched until we had all but the last clues and then the bell rang. The winners were Judith Esland and Jennifer Bell. Next we went into the inner garden to watch an entertainment given by 6B. They combed their hair over their faces and wore masks at the back of their heads. Their clothes were very funny and old fashioned. They did everything backwards. After that we went onto the games field to watch
> another entertainment, given by 6A. This was about George and the Dragon; the dragon was very good; also there was a giant who was prancing about waving a truncheon at St. George. When we went into school the chairman of the governors presented each of us with a Coronation mug. After tea the party ended and we all went home grateful to everyone who helped to give us such a lovely party.

The magazines featured poems composed by the girls but during the 1950s Miss Bull specially requested that poems submitted should not to be about springs or brooks.

Daphne Moorhouse of Lower IVJ tried to break the mould with a poem entitled:-

WESTWOOD SCHOOL

> The thrushes wake at five
> Along the drive;
> Across the copse the cuckoo calls,
> The spreading cedars, under laid
> With pools of dappled shade,
> Stand guardian to the dreaming wall
> Where sunlight softly falls.
> Happily the whole day long

```
A laughing throng
Haunts the green lawns: the sunset chars
As evening droops and draws the light
From windows, that all day long were bright;
And Westwood, beneath a sweep of stars,
Awaits the dawn's gold bars.
```

Another attempt to pen something different was by a girl in Va. She was probably aware of the story of a girl who had fainted while in class and was taken to the sick room and put into bed and forgotten. This room used to be opposite the old library. Emma Massey gave her poem the title *The Forbidden Room:*

```
At Westwood Hall there is an awesome room,
Full of dark shadows, overhung with gloom.
I open the door, with notice, Enter not
Stand there in horror, rooted to the spot
What do I see? Oh fearsome sight to tell!
The vision holds me fast, as by a spell:
No gleam of light streams through the window tall
To set the sunbeams dancing on the wall,
But black, foul shadows creep, and glide away.
I see a still, frail form; I dare not stay
Lest I should break a sick nymph's sweet repose;
I steal away. The sickroom door I close.
```

The magazine recorded the many charities supported by the school. Each form collected for their chosen one each week, this freedom of choice resulted in a very long list with hospitals, children and animals predominating. Typical of the yearly list were: The British Empire Cancer Campaign, The Orthopaedic Hospital at Hartshill, National Association for the Prevention of Tuberculosis, The Pestalozzi Children's Village, Dr. Barnardo's Homes, The Sunshine Home for Blind Babies, NSPCC and Guide Dogs for the Blind.

The total amount of money raised for charities in 1950 was £69.0s.1d. A similar pattern of support was followed in the late 40s, 50s and 60s.

In the war years of 1939-45 the charities supported reflected the war effort and national fund raising schemes such as Aid to Russia Fund, Aid to China Fund, Prisoners of War, Merchant Navy Comforts Fund, St. Dunstan's, and the Soldiers' Sailors' and Air Force Families' Association. The girls of Westwood had responded to the needs of the day and showed that they were aware of the outside world.

As well as collecting for charities there was the weekly collection for National Savings. Many girls bought their 6d and 2/6 stamps so that when they had £1 they could exchange them for a certificate. The activities of the many school societies were well documented and there were many reports on the Inter-Schools Classical Association, the Literary and Debating Society and the Council for Education in World Citizenship. The CEWC was always very popular, not for its speakers or its international themes, but for the fact that meetings were often held in boys' schools!

There were always letters from old girls in the magazines reporting their experiences after leaving Westwood, the majority, by far, were from girls at teacher training college or university and who had been in the sixth form. The following letters also show the delight each girl found in her new environment and gave an insight into life over half a century ago:

Homerton College, Cambridge 1951

Dear Westwood,

I am glad to be writing to you on this warm, sunny day, for Cambridge is most beautiful when the sun shines. You ought to come and see it, and perhaps go punting on the river. I will give you some of the facts about college life that do not get into the college prospectus. We are 'ruled' by a senior student with her deputy and twelve representatives. During the first year here, two of us share a study bedroom on the second floor. We are now used to running up and down fifty nine stairs, but it is

Homerton College Cambridge where
Dorothea Nixon was a student.

better not to forget something. We have a general course which prepares us to teach any subject in a Modern Secondary or Primary School if we are called upon. I do more PT. than I did at school, in a perfectly equipped gymnasium. In the second year we reduce the number of subjects and specialize in one or two. The second year course begins in a fortnight's time, after the first year examinations. These examinations are the first I have done for over a year, but once more I find myself in the throes of revision. Our comparatively short terms and long vacations lead people to believe that we do not work hard. Compared with girls studying for Higher School Certificate we do not, but the work is so different and so much of our time is taken up with lectures, which may go on until ten minutes past five and on Saturday mornings, so that a comparison is not just. After the examinations we shall do a month of our second year course before we go down. I am hoping to study geography and dress designing to an advanced level, and I should have a little more free time.

We have College sports teams which play neighbouring training college teams. We have a big sports field and beautiful college grounds. We are fortunate that our social life is bound up with that of the University, for we can grasp the opportunities that would normally be confined to the University. Cambridge seems to be one of those towns which has everything. Cambridge cannot be fully appreciated until one has spent some time here. Neither does one appreciate home and the former way of life until it is left behind. I should like to pay tribute to the brotherly unity of the University. It is reassuring to see men and women of all religious denominations, colours, races and social levels living and working together in tolerance and harmony. That is the note on which to leave Cambridge.

Goodbye and good luck to you all.
 Dorothea Nixon

University of Durham 1951

Dear Westwood,

I have been asked by a member of your magazine committee to write a letter telling you about Durham. Durham is a quaint place no bigger than Leek. The streets are very narrow and the traffic is very fast. The River Wear flows through the city in the shape of a letter U and in the semi - peninsular are situated the Cathedral, the Castle and the University.

Durham University where
Shirley Hazelhurst was a student

The latter consists of many low buildings, not of one modern red brick whole as one might expect. Indeed one of the chief aims of the University is to keep up traditions and that is why students wear gowns in lectures and in the evenings.

Durham is also different from most Universities in that it is a collegiate. That means that the actual University is split up into six men's and four women's colleges. One of the men's colleges is situated in the castle, and it is not unusual to see a pair of men's trousers flying from the Castle flagpole instead of the conventional flag.

Sport (next to work) is the main interest of the students. Every kind of game is played at some time or other. There is even a women's lacrosse team which challenged the men's hockey team to a 'Lachokey' match.

This being the summer term, most people are working hard for the June examinations, but some still have time for tennis, cricket and the chief sport of Durham, rowing.

There are boat races held each term. So far it has always rained but it is hoped the weather will be fine for the Regatta in June Week, which is a week of pleasure at the end of the term when exams are over (and results are coming out).

I am afraid I must finish this letter with a lot unsaid!

With best wishes
Shirley Hazelhurst

What magazines still exist are in private hands and the authors of this book have been fortunate and privileged to have seen many of the forty or so that were produced at Westwood, plus a number from the Church School days. To all those who contributed from the headmistresses, teachers and pupils, but above all to the editors, thanks are due. Within the magazine pages is captured some of the spirit of Westwood and a wonderful record of days when education was something special for the chosen few.

The Speech Day ceremony in the hall at the Boys' High School 1956.

The Provost Medals awarded annually to the Head Girl at Westwood and the Head Boy at L.H.S.

Chapter 10
Speech Days

In the early years of the school Speech Day had been held in the Town Hall, but with the opening of the Boys' High School in 1939, the occasion was transferred to the Boys' School hall. To accommodate the girls the boys had a holiday.

At the speech day held in January 1944 Sir Francis Joseph presented the prizes. In part of his very humorous address, based on the characters in *Alice in Wonderland,* he spoke of the confusion that arose when he asked the way to the ceremony's venue. *'I arrived in Leek, and asked,"Where is the Girls' High School?" They replied, "It's in the Boys' High School" Then they added, "You see, we are making the Boys' High School respectable for this afternoon. We've turned all the boys out. There's only the caretaker left, and he's busy locking up the coal cellar. That's all they use coal cellars for now, to lock coal up," "But", I said, "How do the girls keep warm?" "Oh they do that*

by clapping their hands together, you may think that they are applauding you, but they won't be, you know, they'll be keeping themselves warm."' (In this period of the war all fuel was scarce, boiler fuel in particular, and heating was usually turned off in the afternoons).

Hilary Ogden first arrived at Westwood, nearly five years after Sir Francis's visit and was very soon involved in a Speech Day. Here she gives a candid account of what it meant to her and the lasting love of music it brought:

Towards the end of the summer term of 1949 I went to school one morning to be

Four smiling Prize Winners in 1954. Left: Dorothy Winterton, Ann Crump, Margaret Beard and Jill Mulliss.

told that I had been accepted at Westwood Hall Girls' High School the following term. My father told me of some of the changes I would find at the High School. These included Speech Days, an unfamiliar term to me at that time. I didn't have long to wait before I experienced my first one at Westwood. The chosen date for 1949 was 11th November, just a few weeks after I had arrived. Westwood did not possess a large hall so the ceremony was held in the Boys' High School.

The school day began as usual at 9am, but at the Boys' High School instead of Westwood. After assembly a rehearsal of the procedures for Speech Day took place. These took the whole of the morning. Much of the time was taken in perfecting the anthems which had been prepared for several weeks in our music lessons. The whole school would sing some of these and others by the choir. After the music, the presentation and receiving of prizes took place, staff member standing in for the guest speaker who would only be present for the actual event in the afternoon. As no dinners were available, the girls living locally would go home for dinner. Those who lived too far away, had to stay in Leek. Many girls who lived locally would take a friend home for a meal. Others ate in town either at The White Hart or Tatton's where I went with my friend, the late Margaret Nadin and her mother. It was a novel experience to eat in a restaurant and I

The detailed programme for 1955

Westwood Hall Girls' High School, Leek

PRIZE GIVING

FEBRUARY 3rd, 1955

Singles : Senior   Bernice Johnson
         Junior   Barbara Walklett

Dramatic Contest :   Upper V

Parents' Cup   Lower VP

Northern Universities Joint Matriculation Board
GENERAL CERTIFICATE OF EDUCATION

June, 1954

AT ORDINARY LEVEL :

Upper Fifth :

Elaine Baggaley
Anne Bainbridge
Wendy Barber
Sheila Barrow
Mary Bass
Margaret Beard
Margaret Beardmore
Edna Bloor
Joan Brocklehurst
Lesley Bullock
Gillian Calvert
Anita Cliff
Jean Chlow
Christine Corbishley
Ann Crump
Janet Dawson
Gwendolyn Daykin
Valerie Edwards
Gillian Frost
Dorothy Hall
Judith Hancock
Mary Harris

Freda Harrison
Gwenyth Hine
Sheila Hudson
Barbara Johnson
Patricia Kent
Mavis Mellor
Ruth Milner
Jean Mottershead
June Mountford
Hilary Ogden
Sylvia Parr
Dorothy Poole
Nora Richards
Josephine Rushton
Norma Sharpe
Jean Shelton
Gabrielle Snow
Marcia Stubbs
Margaret Stubbs
Ann Wardle
Janet Warrington
Gertrude Wilcox

Sixth Form :

Mary Brough
Christina Brunt
Margaret Cartwright
Christine Day
Dorothy Hambleton
Suzanne Hancock

Jean Hodge
Ann Jackson
Sheila Mayers
Beryl Messham
Ann Palmer
Barbara Pickering

AT ADVANCED LEVEL :

Janet Ainsworth
Eileen Beaumont
Miriam Bunker
Alison Felton
Beryl Fisher
Carol Heywood
Bernice Johnson

Rosalind Moorhouse
Jamie Prime
Ruth Stabler
Audrey Thornton
Margaret Wakelin
Catherine Waterhouse

Programme for 1955 showing pupils gaining G.C.E. certificates

PROGRAMME

God Save the Queen

SONGS The Song of the Music Makers - *Martin Shaw* THE SCHOOL
The Kangaroo - *Alec Rowley* UPPER IV, LOWER IV, III

HEAD MISTRESS'S REPORT

THE CHAIRMAN

SONG Deep River - *arr. Hugh S. Roberton* THE CHOIR

PRESENTATION OF PRIZES

The Very Reverend W. S. MACPHERSON, M.A.

SONG When Icicles Hang by the Wall - *R. Vaughan Williams* THE SCHOOL

VOTE OF THANKS

SCHOOL SONG Pioneers - *Martin Shaw* THE SCHOOL

PRIZES

VIa Janet Ainsworth, Eileen Beaumont, Beryl Fisher, Carol Heywood, Bernice Johnson, Rosalind Moorhouse, Margaret Wakelin, Catherine Waterhouse.

VIb Margaret Cartwright, Ann Jackson, Janet Johnston, Elisabeth Spilsbury, Anne Thomas.

Upper V : *Form* Margaret Beard, Edna Bloor, Joan Brocklehurst, Anita Cliff, Ann Crump, Janet Dawson, Mary Harris, Ruth Milner.
Progress Anne Bainbridge, Jean Mottershead, Dorothy Poole, Jean Sheldon, Janet Warrington.

Lower V : *Form* Jennifer Bailey, Pamela Hewitt, Jill Mulliss, Averil Sutton.
Progress Margaret Booth, Marion Lloyd, Marjorie Stannard, Beryl Turner.

Upper IV : *Form* Jean Allcock, Sylvia Birch, Elizabeth Brassington, Phyllis Nicholls, Pat Thomson, Jacqueline Whitwham.
Progress Mavis Harrison, Mavis Heath, Hazel Pointon.

Lower IV : *Form* Monica Booth, Maisie Cliffe, Ann Keates.
Progress Marion Binns, Carolyn Johnson, Jennifer Rider

III : *Form* Christine Ash, Dorothy Hackney, Christine Hulme, Mary Keates, Enid Partington.
Progress Valerie Fowler, Heather Sayer.

The William and Mary Provost Medal : Rosalind Moorhouse
The William Bromfield Memorial Prize : Alison Felton
Reading Prize : Junior (given by the Governors) Judith Pursaill
Senior (,, ,, ,,) Alison Felton
Mathematics : Junior (given by the Governors) Elizabeth Brassington
Senior (given by Miss Carless) Margaret Wakelin

French : (given by Miss Phillipson) Barbara Pickering
Needlework : (given by Miss Martin) Dorothy Winterton
Cookery : (given by Mrs. Hassall) Mavis Harrison, Mavis Heath
Junior History : (given by Miss Griffith) Hazel Pointon
Junior Music : (given by Miss Wardill) Patricia Hopkinson
Junior Scripture : (given by Mr. A. E. Hughes) Jean Allcock
Junior Wild Flower Collections : (given by the Governors) Janice Baxter and Lynne Sheldon

Parents' Guild Prize : Rosalind Moorhouse
The Dr. and Mrs. W. E. Alkins University Leaving Prize : Eileen Beaumont

Old Girls' Scholarship : Alison Felton, Beryl Fisher, Carol Heywood

TROPHIES

Gymnastics : Senior VIa and Lower VP
             Junior IIIR
Hockey : Senior Lower VT
Netball : Senior Upper V
        Junior Lower IVG
Rounders : Senior Upper IVW
          Junior IIIG
Tennis : Form VIB

The many prize winners in 1954.

was impressed when Margaret's mother left a sixpence under the plate for the waitress.

After lunch we returned to the Boys' High School for the official procedures of Speech Day. As a ten year old I was over-awed by the formality of the occasion. This was the one day in the year when the staff wore their academic gowns. The exception was the music mistress who would wear a smart dress or costume. She would be in a prominent position in her role as conductor of the singing. Of all the Speech Days that I attended during my seven years at Westwood, the first one made the greatest impression on me. It went without saying that we were expected to be a credit to the school and that nothing short of perfection would be acceptable. As far as I was aware, this was achieved.

When all were seated the official proceedings began with the singing of The National anthem followed by a song that had been much practised beforehand. In my early years our music mistress was Mrs. Heath and she favoured traditional choral music by composers such as Bach, Handel and Purcell. After Mrs Heath retired Miss Wardill took over the post of music mistress and introduced some more modern works by Britten, Thiman and Elgar. At my first Speech day in 1949 the school sang 'Wake, Wake for Night is Flying' and the choir sang Handel's' lovely Peace.' Both themes have remained with me to this day, as have many more of the anthems that I was introduced to on Speech Days.

The first speech of the afternoon was made by the Headmistress. She reported on events and activities in the past year. The Chairman of the Governors then welcomed the speaker and thanked him for agreeing to give the address and to distribute the prizes. The guest speaker was usually a person of high-standing in the academic world. During my time at Westwood two former headmistresses performed this duty. Miss ER de Sausmarez attended in 1951 and Mrs A. Hearn (formerly Miss EM Bull) in 1956. A learned address which usually had moral under-tones for the benefit of the girls preceded the presentation of prizes, trophies and certificates.

These were carefully arranged in order on the table on the stage. Many had been given to the school by former governors, staff and pupils. They included the William and Mary Provost medal, the William Bromfield memorial prize, the Dr. and Mrs W.E. Alkins University leaving prize, Miss Phillipson's prize for French, The Old Girls Awards, the Parents' Guild prize, Mrs Hassall's prize for cookery, Miss Martin's prize for needlework, the form prizes and the progress prizes. The captains of the netball, rounders and tennis teams collected the trophies on behalf of their teams, followed by a trophy to the winners of the dramatic competition. Finally the 'O' level and 'A' level certificates were presented. The whole occasion was a demonstration of behaviour at its best.

A vote of thanks to the guest speaker would be proposed and seconded by members of the Board of Governors. The speaker would respond and would request a day's holiday for the girls in celebration of Speech day. The school would sing the final anthem before Speech Day came to a close with the singing of the school song 'Pioneers' set to music by Martin Shaw.

There were more than forty Speech Days in the Grammar School years when Westwood was on show and always acquitted itself well. In the memories of pupils and teachers these occasions still loom large. Programmes for the ceremonies confirm that little changed over the years. This was part of the beauty of that one day in the year which was so strictly formal and so predictable. For young girls it was a day like no other in the year. The addresses may have been forgotten but the songs and the music and the pomp remain, always to be treasured.

Miss Telford with prefects 1960

Miss Telford with prefects 1961.
Back: Angela Walley, Marjorie Haycock, Vivienne Emmott, Hilary Bollington, Dorothy Mountford, Janet Tryhall.
Front: Joy Rowlinson, Hilary Kershaw, Miss Telford, Freda Hine, Jillian Griffiths, Marie Povey.

Chapter 11
Miss Telford Headmistress January 1956-August 1976

In the autumn term of 1955 five candidates were interviewed for the permanent post of headmistress. Miss M. Telford BA was appointed as from the first of January 1956 and she was to stay for two decades.

Miss Telford

The new Headmistress faced a number of serious problems as she took up her new office. Firstly there was the destination of school leavers and what higher and further educational establishments they might attend or what jobs they would enter in the world of industry and commerce. There was a consensus of opinion that girls did not achieve their true potential in external exams or the world after school.

In her first two reports to governors Miss Telford highlighted a trend that had been at Westwood since its birth. Too few girls went to university and a large number usually well into double figures went to Teacher Training Colleges. The largest group went into clerical or secretarial posts. There were differences here, as girls who had at least one year in the sixth form went into banking and those who left at sixteen took up clerical jobs. A decade later the largest number of leavers entered the textile

Miss Telford with prefects.
Standing: Joy Rowlinson, Jennifer Slack, April Johnson, Enid Partington, Ann Hemming, Ann Brammer.
Sitting: Irene Adams, Hilary Bowman (Head Girl), Miss Telford, Pat Baigent, Jean Hayward.

Miss Lakin's form 1962.

Form photograph 1962.

Miss Beck's form 1962.

Miss Eros' form.

industry, seven of those going to work at Job White. Twenty girls went into shop work, with Woolworths being the most popular destination. The changes that had taken place were not perhaps what was wanted or envisaged. The whole purpose and basis of grammar school education came into question and moves were made both nationally and locally to initiate a system of comprehensive education.

Unsuitable, inadequate and poor accommodation had been a problem since the opening of Westwood in 1921 and, so far, little had been done to improve matters. The depression of the inter-war years, the war period and the austerity years that followed may have been partly to blame but now there was a chance to improve matters. New accommodation was badly needed and it took time to put such buildings on site. Westwood was not built as a school, it was a family home and when the authorities decided to use the building as a school there were many problems to overcome.

As the number of pupils grew, accommodation was quite an issue. There was no proper gym, no showers, no proper laboratories or a dining hall. There was no room for the whole school to gather together for assemblies. However the girls had accepted things as they were. Over the years they hardly noticed the difficulties but simply got on with everyday life, living it to the full.

It took two years of hard work by the Headmistress to get any improvements in accommodation and initially these were only minor. The hearth was removed from the entrance hall/gym. This gave an extra 12 square feet P.E. There was a growing list of requests for more and better accommodation .The teaching of art was hampered as the room used would only hold twenty girls. More girls were studying science so a new science lab was also needed. By 1959 plans were being drawn up for alterations and extensions to Westwood. In the meantime the staff staircase up to the attics was completely repaired and three old, dangerous chimney stacks were removed.

In 1961 work had commenced in earnest on the new additions to the school. The increase in numbers had made this essential. The architects and surveyors who had inspected the school promised that the new buildings would not detract from the charm of the original building. When the work started some of the old buildings were taken down. In her address at the speech day of 1961 Miss Telford said that the building operations were now well advanced and expressed her gratitude to the staff and to the pupils for their perseverance and co-operation in the school, especially when some of the corridors had been blocked and cloakrooms and form rooms had disappeared. By the beginning of 1962 the new cloakrooms were ready and the new laboratories were being finished.

The speech day of 1963 was very different from its predecessors, as it was held at Westwood in the newly built hall and not at the Boys' High School. It was held in the summer term and marked the official opening of the new extensions - the hall laboratories and other specialist rooms. In fact it had to be held twice! The demand for seats could not be met, even with the new hall, so the ceremony was held on two consecutive days, Thursday 16th and 17th May. The chairman of the Education Committee declared the extensions officially open and handed the responsibility for them over to the governors. The School Magazine's editorial of 1963 reported on the building work that had been going on. Elizabeth Sal argued that in the final analysis, the upset was well worth it:

The extensions have at last been completed. Now we know that the few years of inconvenience and noise have all been well worth it. Already we can hardly imagine being without the new rooms and there are greater opportunities for all the girls. Bright displays throughout the school show that the girls are very enthusiastic about the improved art facilities. The new hall, which is also a large gymnasium, makes it possible for the whole school to meet together and now this happens every morning for prayers.

First team hockey 1957.

Staffordshire Schools' Champions 1960.

School tennis team 1963.

Netball team.

Staff hockey team 1960.
Miss June Wrathall second from left front row,
with Miss Betty Ward next to her at the end.
Mr Round and Mr Goodacre are on the back row.

By 1964 plans were made to provide a bus park on land at the top of the front drive, with a new caretaker's house nearby. At the same time plans were set in motion to extend the school playing field. In 1966 Mr Plant at Westwood farm agreed to sell to the authority the 0.20 acre of land required to give access to the site of the proposed bus park at the eastern side of the school building. It was also proposed that a new school should be constructed nearby. It was to be known as St Edward's Hall. At the beginning of 1976 the caretaker moved into the newly built school house.

Miss Telford continued the tradition of her predecessors in celebrating the school's foundation. In 1961, the 40th birthday was marked by a thanksgiving service at St. Edward's Parish Church. In the following year there was another service but this time a joint service, for Westwood and the Boys' High School to mark the beginning of the new term.

Miss Telford also decided that the school uniform needed some changes. She introduced new blazers for the sixth formers with silver bands around the lapels and cuffs. The ties became more fashionable with their diagonal stripes and the summer uniform was altered to green gingham dresses which were much more attractive.

Drama and music had always been an important part of school life. There were visits to to see *The Comedy of Errors* at Stratford, *Henry V* at Leek, *Romeo and Juliet* at the Opera House in Manchester, *The Merchant of Venice* at the Boy's High School and Lichfield Cathedral for a performance of Bach's *Passion according to St. Matthew*.

Over the years numerous plays and productions were staged at Westwood. John Milton's *Comus* was performed in the grounds at the front of the School in the late 1950s. In this play the Duke of Bridgewater decided to reside at Ludlow Castle where his three eldest children were to join him. On the way there the two boys became separated from their sister and she was found by the wicked enchanter, Comus. However it all ended happily when everyone was reunited. The play was performed outside in front of the school building especially for the parents.

Dorothy Mountford (Mrs Davies) took part in the production:

I was in the chorus and we were seated amongst the bushes in the paddock area. We had practised our parts well and we were really looking forward to the play. All went well until one of the girls fell off her chair and disappeared into the bushes. We struggled to stifle our giggles, but the more we tried the more we doubled up with laughter and completely missed our cue. The result was slight chaos and Miss Lakin was not amused.

In March 1960 there was Smetana's *The Bartered Bride*. The principal parts were played by Irene Adams, Jennifer Simpson and Elizabeth Salt. The main boys' parts were taken by Tony Gallimore, Ian Stuart, Russell Pedlar, Christopher Moorhouse and Cameron Howes with a supporting cast of over fifty people. As usual it was held in the Boys' High School and the performances were so highly successful that many people were disappointed because they were unable to book seats.

At the end of the summer term in 1965 Westwood Hall Girls' High school ceased to exist. New accommodation had been built to be used by the newly created comprehensive school. It was the end of an era. At the beginning of the autumn term there were now 483 pupils consisting mainly of 339 ex grammar school girls, 113 girls from the Milner Girls' school and 24 from the Leek Parish Church Secondary Modern.

The girls who had started at Westwood before 1965 were to complete their grammar school courses. St.Edward's Church of England Junior School was built near the woods and later when

The Bartered Bride March 1960.

The Bartered Bride March 1960.

further re-organisation took place it became known as New Hall and became part of the Westwood complex catering for 13 to 19 year olds.

By 1969 the school was fully comprehensive, and fully co-educational by 1971 when the intake of 1966 reached the sixth form. Miss Phillipson retired in the summer of 1962 and sadly died two years later. In 1969 Miss Beck retired after 44 years dedicated service to the school. She had certainly witnessed some changes in her time. Mr Howson the caretaker retired in 1973.

In 1975 Miss Telford decided it was time to resign. She had steered the school through many changes, from a girls' grammar to the comprehensive school. The whole school gathered in the Westwood Hall for the final assembly when she was presented with gifts from the head boy and the head girl.

The post was advertised and Mr George Wiskin from the Sir Leo Schultz High School, Humberside was appointed as the first headmaster at Westwood.

Memories of Westwood Girls' High Schools later years, recalled by pupils and two teachers.

Hilary Fox (Mrs. Brown)

I well remember sitting in the hall at Primary School taking the 11 plus. Everyone around me had been bribed with visions of bikes, a scooter or roller skates, I was just expected to pass. After all, what greater accolade could one's family have, than a daughter at Westwood High School for Girls?

So I passed and dressed in the green uniform purchased at Bayleys the outfitters. The day in September arrived. Bearing in mind that at that time I lived at the farthest point in the town from the school, there were no school buses apart from those which brought the girls from the rural areas, I caught the town bus and got off at the lodge and walked up the long drive, and then suddenly there I was at Westwood. The grey brown stone was warmed by the September sun. Inside the smell of polish emanated from the creaking staircases and floorboards. Outside were the manicured lawns and gravel pathways. Some of the staff looked severe in their flowing black gowns. It was like every girls' school in every comic devoured over the years, but secretly thought didn't exist. You wanted to be there with girls called Pip, Bunty and Jinty and to join in all their jolly escapades. It was like Hogworts but without the magic! We had to learn unintelligible subjects like Latin, Algebra, Geometry, - spiffing, jolly hockey sticks, what fun!

After a week reality set in. The timetable was relentless -1 hour for lunch taken over two sittings, and 3 hours of homework every night, not to mention the 3 mile walk to school there and back if you missed the bus.

However, as time went on and feeling our feet we began to bend the rules, if only slightly. We had forays to the cellars, which we were convinced were haunted, and up on the roof. This tended to be an end of term event as we tried to see who could make it before we were caught. Someone brought Woodbines which we smoked in the woods when we should have been at a tennis match and we returned looking greener than the court. We hitched up our skirts to mini length, after all it was the sixties, pinned our porkpie hats on the back of our heads and backcombed our hair over them.

Even to eat sweets or chips in the street was strictly forbidden according to the rules. After all we were supposed to act like young well bred ladies all the time!

We performed plays and one I particularly remember was Alice through the Looking Glass. Myself and three other girls, all being the smallest in the class, were dressed in tutus and had to pretend to be daisies. Bored with the whole thing we began to nudge each other and whisper throughout the entire performance, only to be given extra points for ingenuity and acting ability! Foiled again!

I was caught once climbing through the music room window by Miss Ward. I thought it was one of my friends telling me off so I told her to shut up! That earned me 100 lines of 'I shall not be rude to a teacher', done in secret in my bedroom, so that mother would not know of the shame I had brought on the family. I trust that when I become a prefect my reign will be more benign. We had Speech Days which brought endless days of rehearsals, best bib and tucker, and teachers in caps and gowns. I was envious of all the girls getting prizes, something I could never achieve.

Just three friends.

I remember school trips, such as going to Manchester to see 'Romeo and Juliet' and being escorted to a Wimpey Bar by teachers swearing us to secrecy. But the cruise and skiing trips was beyond my parents' means and I never participated.

Looking back it must have been difficult for teachers who had been at Westwood for a long time, to have to deal with slightly rebellious 1960s teenagers! Times were changing, ours was the last year that was all girls before the school became comprehensive and the era of the grammar school was gone forever. My mother had been a pupil when Miss de Sausmarez was headmistress and she had a saying that was quite radical for her time, 'Educate a girl and you educate a family', a sentiment that still holds true today.

Miss Sheila Bettany a teacher 1961:

The first time that I went to Westwood (apart from playing hockey matches whilst at the Orme) and meeting Miss Telford was in February 1961. I was to be interviewed for a Chemistry teaching post - starting in September. It was a snowy February day, and I walked up from Burton Street, past the lodge and up the drive - it seemed a very long way! When I was taken into Miss Telford's office (complete with an open coal fire) her welcome was kind and she put me at ease. She talked to me about the post that I was applying for, and prepared me for what to expect later in the day. The Head of science, Derek Goodacre, showed me the existing labs, and explained that soon there was to be an extension, including new labs. Derek took me around the school and I was interviewed by the Chairman of Governors and Miss Telford later in the day. I was to meet Stan Hurst who was interviewed in May, and Derek, Stan and I were together in the Science department for over 25 years. (Miss Telford gave us space to run the

Last day at school.

Presentation to the Music Mistress.

The prefects with Miss Telford in 1960.

The prefects with Miss Telford in 1959.
Back: Judith Blackhurst, Marian Binns, Diane Clarke, Maisie Cliffe, Caroline Johnson.
Front: Pat Baigent, Pat Thompson, Miss Telford, Freda Parker, Vilma Wright.

Department, and was only involved in syllabus decisions).

Since then, when other staff were interviewed and appointed, I felt that Miss Telford was a shrewd judge of people's abilities and strengths, and over the years she brought together a good team. This was especially so, when we changed to an 11-18 comprehensive and mixed school.

At first we held our staff meetings in the old staff rooms in the attics, but as the new school buildings were added we moved into the old library and the sixth form moved into the attics. There were contacts with the parents in the Parent Guild and a committee was formed to arrange events at the school - garden parties and fund raising events later. I was involved with that committee as well as being responsible for Pastoral Care and later for administering the GCSE examinations.

In 1965 we were 'reorganised' into the Comprehensive Education System, and later the Middle school was set up. Miss Telford then appointed three deputies, Derek Goodacre, June Wrathall and later Malcolm Brewin, who had had experience with the house system. A house system was developed and the names of the different houses were the names of families and places that had had connections with Westwood's history: Stafford, Lichfield, Davenport and Johnson. It was a testing time of change, but Miss Telford was able to cope well with it all, with resilience (and excellent support from her staff). The staff coped well with the changes. Miss Lakin surprised everyone, because after many years teaching the grammar school girls she adjusted very well to coping with the boys. We were always blessed with good ancillary staff appointments too. The secretaries, caretakers, ground staff lab. assistants all seemed to feel that they were part of a team which of course helped in the smooth running of the school and was due to the influence of the Head.

Miss Betty Ward a teacher 1956-1981:

I came to Westwood in 1956 and stayed 25 year before moving to the Middle School in 1981. I came from a lively and very academic girls' school in Preston and I couldn't believe the change. My first impression of the building and grounds and the view from the hockey field was of the great beauty of it all a feeling that lasted 25 years in spite of the great expansion of the school. All the alterations have preserved the country house appearance. In 1956 I didn't think there would be many more than 250 girls with a very small sixth form. Girls came from a considerable distance, some on school buses, some on the train, many having to walk up Burton Street. Some from Endon and beyond on the service bus then walking up the back drive: a rough track over what is now the Wallbridge estate.

Inside school we were quite cramped for space, although some of the classrooms were delightful with elaborate plaster ceilings and fine fireplaces and large windows with glorious views. The science labs were just classrooms with some Bunsen burners and test tubes etc. You went out and across a narrow bridge to get to the art room. There was no where big enough for the whole school to meet together, so every day there were two assemblies, one in the back hall with the minstrel's gallery and one in what became the music room: a beautifully panelled room. Prize giving was always held at Leek High School, which was then situated in Westwood Road, where the boys had a hall which could hold all of us plus visitors. Rehearsals for the singing by the whole school, including 'Pioneers' took priority over everything else. Some sixth formers occasionally went the High School for lessons and joint productions were held there. In my first year it was Gilbert and Sullivan. We had no gym and

SCHOOL PHOTOGRAPH 1957.

SCHOOL PHOTOGRAPH 1963.

SCHOOL PHOTOGRAPH 1963.

used the entrance hall. Girls would run down the corridor vault over the horse and land outside the front door!

The timetable was organised with 5 lessons in a morning and 2 in the afternoon and ensured that all staff had a free afternoon. Those whose homes were a long way away got Friday off where possible. I think this system lasted possibly 4 or 5 years till the time table became very complicated.

In 1956 there were no cars in the courtyard. Only two staff had cars and they went into the garage. The rest of us lived in digs in walking distance of the school, a few at home towards the Potteries coming in by bus. There was no need to close in snow on account of teachers not being in, although occasionally the school buses were called out early when the weather was bad.

It was a small staff but an exceptionally friendly staff. We had a set of rooms in the attics, which we were informed were unsafe for any girls to be allowed up there. There were long tables on which we could leave our books or sit at and work. Another room had comfortable chairs for relaxing in or drinking tea, all removed from the general noise of the school, which was left to the member of staff on duty to cope with. I found many of the country girls very reluctant to engage in discussion and express their opinions. It was an interesting change when we went comprehensive and co-ed. The boys were often lazier than the girls but much more forthcoming in class. I can remember in my first weeks thinking I really ought to stay 4 years and here I am still in Leek. Things changed without my needing to move.

A few girls went to university but before the expansion of the building societies, there was not much for girls leaving at 16. Fortunate ones went into a bank or one of the mill offices, otherwise it was work in the mills or shops. Those leaving with 'A' levels usually went into nursing or teaching. Westwood gave me 25 happy years and most of my friends today are still those I met in the staffroom there.

Anne Bainbridge

It is difficult today to appreciate the isolation of Westwood Hall in the early days of the school, situated out to the west of the town in open countryside. The decision to locate a school in such an isolated spot was made miles away at Stafford although pressure was also applied by a few people in Leek who had a financial interest in the sale of the estate.

Westwood would remain isolated for the next three decades. No matter from which direction you approached the school there was always a long walk.

Pupils who lived seven miles to the south west who were successful in the 11+ examination would find themselves allocated to grammar schools in Leek. Most knew where Leek was though few had visited the town. But where was Westwood Hall?

Girls who came to School on the service bus along the A53 from Baddeley Green, or Bagnall, could alight at the bottom of Ladderedge at the bottom lodge and walk to school up the lonely back drive through the fields and copses bordering it. There were no houses along the drive until the top lodge three quarters of a mile away at the gateway to the hall. If a girl was late for school, or had to leave early, the walk could be very uncomfortable.

An alternative route was to alight at Burton Street, walk up the hill, then across the recreational ground, then turn left into Westwood Road and up the drive to School. Girls coming by train would follow this route.

The front drive was like the back drive, there were no houses, apart from a small cluster near the Westwood Road Lodge. If the girls had to remain behind at school for some reason, particularly during the winter months when it went dark early, there were no lights.

For those girls who lived in the centre of town or out on the Buxton road the journey would involve a walk of over a mile - for decades there were no regular service buses along Westwood Road to the Lodge. Some special buses brought girls from outlying villages, they were the fortunate ones, but they lost out as they could not stay for after school activities.

The isolation of Westwood was gradually lost in the second half of the century, with the housing development in the area between the top lodge and the Hall and later the larger development on the Wallbridge Estate, together of course with the advent of private transport.

Margaret Mason 1960-1967 (Mrs Bowyer)

Several events come to mind: our skiing holiday at Axams near Innsbruck and a geography field trip to Borth, great adventures. We were also lucky to go on short courses to Manchester and Keele Universities to study English and Allingham Hall near Shrewsbury for History. We had day trips to science fairs at Birmingham University and a college near Coventry where we used an electron microscope, and several trips to the Victoria Theatre in Stoke.

In my time the uniforms were green and red, with green pork pie hats. School dinners were a must, no going home at lunch time. My mother remembered the old school desks from the old Boys' School on Clerk Bank. They were still there in our second year form in the attic room 1961-62. My antique desk had 'ancient' graffiti.

On a few occasions Miss Telford had to lecture the school at morning assembly about misdemeanours. There should be no need for a rule stating that pupils were to keep off the roof, she told us. The caretaker had left the hatch on the side wall of the stairs unlocked up to the second floor chemistry lab. Some opportunist pupils had found their way through it onto the roof!

Another lecture involved a teacher's missing mini. It had eventually been found hidden behind a wall. Miss Telford appealed to the culprits to own up.

Birthdays in the sixth form were for a time celebrated with cider until senior staff confiscated several bottles and at the same time rumbled the trick of eating oranges to mask the smell of cider. Not many minutes later raucous laughter was heard from the staff room above.

The 1960s saw the Beatles, John F. Kennedy and the Moon exploration. Westwood saw extensive building work with a new assembly hall and science block appearing. We heard that Miss Telford had words with the site manager and asked him to stop his men chatting to the girls. He retorted 'Can you stop your girls talking to my men'.

Miss Telford assured us that Westwood would remain a grammar school; but then she spoke of the school always having a comprehensive ethos. As I moved into the VIth form we became a comprehensive school. The school certainly lost a lot of its decorum for a while.

I remember that Mr Goodacre our Physics master was very keen that we should learn one important electrical skill. He said as future housewives we ought to be able to change an electric plug and not have to wait for the man of the house to do it!

I also remember that we were encouraged to do charitable work - 'Good will doing service' was the motto. I organised UNICEF Christmas cards one year.

Chapter 12
Reflections

In more than four decades, over three thousand girls received a very special kind of education at Westwood, from its opening in 1921 to the change to the more egalitarian comprehensive system of the 1960s. Since then, in celebration of its unique ethos, there have been a number of reunions of old girls and teachers.

For special anniversaries, such as the 50th and 75th years, plaques and mugs, usually in the traditional school green have been produced. A picture of Westwood Hall was always the main feature of such memorabilia. Those attending these reunions would wander the grounds and buildings, remembering the characters and events of the past. With great affection they would cast their eyes on the old hall itself. It still stands there, now showing signs of fatigue after standing proudly against the elements for nearly two centuries.

Diamond Jubilee plaque.   A specially designed plaque by I.A. Johnson

Former pupils walking through the old building will still feel its Victorian aura as they again step on its wooden and tiled floors. They will peek through its tiny windows and feel the panelled walls as they did in years before. They will gaze in wonder at the magnificent fireplace and the striking picture of the school's first headmistress, Miss de Sausmarez. They will feel that this building of their memories is perhaps smaller than when they first remembered it. The farm buildings seem much closer to the school as does the summer house.

They will be shocked to find the old bike shed now displays works of art; that the route down the back drive is now hard to trace through a modern housing estate, even though they once walked it a thousand times or more. They will find the front drive has survived, though it is now lined with houses. Thankfully the lodge on Westwood Road is little changed and the one on Newcastle Road, now extended, looks even grander. The pond has railings around it and what of the large garden where so many pleasant hours were spent growing vegetables for the kitchen

40th Reunion.

Reunion

L to R: Murtle Sales, Sheila Towle, Gladys Sidley, ? Cynthia Malbon, Jennifer Slack, Julia Maskery, Anne Sharrett, Joy Rowlinson, Mary Keats, Elaine Ward, Dorothy Nattell, Jean Haywood & Enid Partington.

65th Reunion.

75th Reunion
L to R: Margaret Beard, Jean Hodge, Ann Jackson, Anne Bainbridge, Catherine Steele, Evelyn Briggs, Freda Harrison, Janet Dawson and Joan Brocklehurst.

75th Reunion Lunch.

during the war years and thereafter? It has disappeared.

There are things new and modern like a most fascinating glass structure attached to the main building providing much needed room and light. The fine hard tennis courts are still there but the grass ones have disappeared. If visitors take a narrow path near the wood and walk away from, and out of sight of the much loved old building, they will find the large New Hall. It has been built in light grey moorland stone that contrasts strangely with the hues of the old Westwood School.

Conversations at such gatherings are more about fondly remembered friends and teachers and about the lessons and studies. There are tears and nostalgia with memories shared, but there is always one comment heard often, *'I am so glad I attended Westwood.'* We leave it to former pupils to crystallize their thoughts and memories of our school.

Rhoda Edwards & Barbara Rawlingson recorded their memories in a poem.

LAST TERM

When Westwood we have left behind,
When we have left the Hall
What memories shall we bring to mind,
What shall we best recall?

The stately building, mellow, red,
The Avenue of trees,
The skylark's singing overhead,
Down drifting on the breeze.

The Churnet flowing down below,
Its banks fresh and green,
Its whispering waters, winding slow
Through pleasant country scene.

We will remember every one,
But better still, we think,
Recall the laughter and the fun ñ
The fingers stained with ink.

Joan Brocklehurst brings back more recent memories of friends and places:

Westwood may not have been my first choice as a high school, but I have always been so thankful that it is where I ended up. Not only did I have wonderful friends, and an interesting and very useful education, but I lived out those years in one of the most beautiful settings imaginable. Many of us who were at Westwood together have kept in touch over the years, and when we are together we reminisce and laugh about all our experiences there, both good and bad! The school has now changed from all-girls to a mixed college for sixth formers. In 1997 we had a marvellous reunion to celebrate over 75 years of Westwood as a school. In the packed auditorium, that had been built in the location of the outdoor toilets. We stood to sing our school song for the very last time together. Few needed the words on the handouts; they were indelibly etched in memory. We had always sung this hymn at the end of each term and year, with the last year in particular meaning so much to all of us. Mrs Heath, the music teacher, had always made sure that we knew when to breathe and how to pronounce the words clearly - and her perpetual legacy of great timing was to be heard on the reunion day. As the old hymn filled the auditorium, a cold shiver went right down my spine; how impressive it was and what a unifying sound after so many years. Although the words were taken from a poem by an American poet, Walt Whitman, extolling Christian pioneers in the New World, those words meant just as much to all of us, as pupils left Westwood for the last time and headed out into the modern world, full of opportunities for the life ahead of us.

> *All the past we leave behind*
> *We take up the task eternal*
> *And the burden and the lesson*
> *Conquering, holding, daring, venturing*
> *So we go our unknown way*
> *Pioneers, Oh pioneers.*

Westwood has had a tremendous influence on so many young lives. Major changes have taken place and more will follow but the spirit and ethos of Westwood will live on in the hearts of those who remember it forever.

The Fire of July 1983

It was very early Friday morning PC Derek Swan, who was on routine patrol, spotted the fire at Westwood Hall and immediately summoned the fire brigade. It seemed likely that the fire had started in the secretary's office on the ground floor and quickly spread to other areas including entrance hall and staircase. Thick smoke hampered the fire brigade's efforts to control the blaze and many rooms suffered smoke damage. It took 60 firemen from six stations over eight hours to extinguish the fire. The *Evening Sentinel* was quick to get the story into print and on Friday 29th July had a head line in large bold black type that proclaimed BLAZE RIPS THROUGH HISTORIC LEEK SCHOOL.

The article quoted the headmaster on the extent of the damage; all pupils had been informed that there would be no school on the last day of term. He was confident that school would open after the summer holiday on September 8th.

There was much speculation over the cause of the fire. Had there been a burglary that had gone wrong? Was it arson? Was it an electrical fault? The police carried out door to door enquiries but did not comment on the likely motive for or source of the blaze.

The news of the fire and the damage caused was quickly spread by the local paper, radio and T.V. Many of those who knew and loved the building feared the worst. There were many unanswered questions. What was the extent of the fire and water damage and would the building and its furnishings be sympathetically repaired and restored and at what cost?

The County Council, acting on advice from a number of interested organisations, decided that no matter how difficult the restoration might be, work should commence as soon as possible. It was essential that the hall was restored to its former grandeur

A Leek firm of architects Hulme, Upright and Partners was engaged to oversee the work. They started with an appeal for photographs, prints and drawings of the interior of the building, so essential for the delicate and intricate work ahead. Fortunately former pupils were able to provide some photographs and sketches. Details of the ornate ceiling and certain wooden carvings were specifically requested, and the ornamental ceilings were reconstructed by apprentices at Cauldon College in Stoke-on-Trent. There was sufficient wall panelling unaffected by the blaze

The fire under control.

Start of a new term September 1983 students survey the damage.

to allow copies to be made. The stained glass window on the staircase was reinstated and the ornamental cast iron radiators were obtained from an old county council building.

As well as restoration to the ground floor, work was undertaken on ten rooms on the upper floor. The restoration work was very successfully undertaken by J.A. Bailey and Sons of Cheadle at a cost of £108,500 met mainly by the insurers. It was to be a year of intense activity before the old hall could be brought back into use.

Mr. George Wiskin, headmaster at the time of the fire, recalled the events.

I was roused in the early hours of Friday 29th July 1983 by the caretaker, to be told that the school was on fire. This was not the first time I had been called out at night for an emergency but this was clearly the most serious.

On arrival I found the Police and the Fire Service labouring to tackle a blaze in the secretary's office on the left of the main entrance. To our horror the flames spread alarmingly to the entrance hall and our fear was that soon the roof would be alight. Anxiety increased when water pressure in the fire hydrant became feeble. Fortunately highly athletic firemen got hoses down the bank of Plant's farm, into the River Churnet, and enough water was pumped up to the school to contain the threat. By the light of day the danger of complete destruction was over and only smoke and steam mingled and infected the air. Tea was brewed on the lawn to revive the fire fighters and the anxious crowd relaxed.

The next day it became possible to inspect the damage. The fire had started in a waste paper bin in the office, ignited by two intruders discarding a lighted brand on leaving the building with a few sweets and crisps. They were identified, found guilty of arson and served a time in detention. The one Westwood lad involved returned contrite and completed his studies in the Sixth Form. Sadly he died several years later.

The damage was most severe in the oak panelled entrance hall, as it was gutted. Flames also reached the splendid ceiling of the nearby classroom and smoke penetrated throughout most corridors and rooms. The Local Education Authority showed its worth with remarkable speed. Their historic buildings architect was put on the job and, within weeks, plans were in place to renovate the building to a high specification, confounding those who thought that skilled workers capable of such craftsmanship were no longer around.

And teaching had to go on! Emergency meetings sorted out the mess, classes were relocated, supplies and equipment replaced, staff used the Senior Study as their base and in no time learning was underway again. In fact exam results improved the following summer!

Reconstruction took a year and the results were impressive. All the oak panelling was copied and shone with a brilliance last seen in 1851 when Westwood Hall was opened. Even the wonderful oak corbels on the staircase were restored and ceilings replastered by experts. The 1960s partitions that had formed the secretary's office, and had disfigured the entrance hall, were removed, giving a grand space for many memorable future receptions and exhibitions. Even wicked thoughts began to arise: was it possible we benefited from the arson? What is certain is that the emergency services, teaching and support staff and the Local Education Authority worked wonderfully together to restore one of finest buildings around for pupils of all abilities and kinds to enjoy their school days.

The year after the fire a special ceremony was held. One hundred guests were invited to attend, including the Chairman of the Staffordshire Moorlands District Council, Mr. Don Machin, the

The facilities available in the much extended College.

Facilities Available

The main types of rooms and facilities that can be hired are as follows:

- Old Hall and New Hall halls
- The Sixth Form Centre
- New Hall Gymnasium
- The Dance Studio
- Classrooms
- Astro Turf Pitch
- Cricket Pitch
- Football Pitches
- Hockey Pitches
- Rugby Pitch
- Conference Facilities
- Weddings
- Extensive Car Parking Facilities

An aerial view of Westwood College and the farm.

Town Mayor, Mr. Robert Baker, and representatives of all the firms involved in the work as well as the actual craftsmen. Mr. Alan Crawford, the Chairman of the Victorian Society re-opened the Hall and stated that the beautifully restored area was now fully integrated into the school and would help Westwood meet the educational demands of the future.

The College Now and in the Future

The 11 to 18 Selective Girls' School which functioned for over four decades was replaced by a co-educational comprehensive college with an age range of 13 to18. The College has more than twice the number of students than the High School had and it certainly has more accommodation and specially designed facilities. The name has changed over the years to the Westwood High School and then to Westwood College.

The most recent visit to the College by Ofsted inspectors was in 2007 and they were most lavish in their praise.

Westwood College is an outstandingly effective school. The headteacher's belief in the importance of inclusion is exceptionally strong; he communicates this clearly to the whole community and it permeates all he does.

The very high quality of the curriculum and the care, guidance and support students receive result in outstanding personal development. Students recognise they are well treated. In response, their behaviour is calm and mature and they treat each other and staff with respect.

The College carries on the good work of educating the teenagers of the Leek area for the world of work and a place in society just as its predecessor did in the earlier part of last century.

The College is opening its doors not only to students but to the population in general. The outside world is being invited to use the wonderful venues and many facilities. An application was made in October 2010 to be allowed for permission to hold weddings.

In a small way the use of the Hall has come full circle. Initially it was the province of the privileged, the Bagnalls, Trenthams and Vanes, then the Davenports, Robinsons and Johnsons who would enjoy the many facilities the estate had to offer. There would have been receptions, games and weddings. Now the Hall's grand buildings and grounds are open to all.

New entrance near to old back door.

A painting of Westwood by ex pupil, Norma Jones.

The Old Hall set out for a wedding reception.